IGNITING THE
LEADING
LADY
IN YOU

DR. HALENE GIDDENS

ISBN: 978-1-7321277-3-9

FOR MORE INFORMATION CONTACT:

760-951-8500

www.destinychristiancenter.org

Cover art by Fred T. Williams Brand LLC

Table of Contents

Foreword

With great joy and honor, I write these words to introduce to some and present to others the special grace upon the life of Dr. Halene Marie Giddens. She is an undeniable voice who has been given an incredible gift to the body of Christ for this present day.

Dr. Halene's ability to empower and teach Leading Ladies comes from her own purpose and posture, serving with me as her husband in the Pastorate and now as the First Lady of the Destiny International Ministerial Alliance (D.I.M.A.) Organization for over the last 25 years.

Now, what we've all been waiting for, her first book, Igniting The Leading Lady In You, is a must-read for all God's daughters with a desire to unlock and fulfill their true purpose in life.

In its pages, Dr. Halene reveals what's been lying dormant in every one of God's beautiful creations, placed in them from the foundation of the world. You will discover who you really are, the diamonds hidden on the inside, it takes time, the characteristics of the Leading Lady, and the faith it takes, just to name a few topics.

I'm persuaded this book will be a vital tool for every

one of God's daughters in pursuit of their divine design and destiny. Once you open these pages, you will clearly see God has anointed Dr. Halene and given her this specific assignment that will *Ignite The Leading Lady In You!*

Bishop Jesse J. Giddens
Destiny Christian Center, Victorville, California
Destiny International Ministerial Alliance (D.I.M.A)

Endorsement

gniting The Leading Lady In You is a must-have for every
woman that will dare to go beyond being "Just A Woman"
to being developed into a "Woman With A Purpose." Dr.
Halene Marie Giddens has captured the potential deep within
the heart of every woman who wants to make a difference in
her life and the Kingdom of God. She lets us know that you are
never too young or too old to spark the leader within.

In the day we live in, a book of this caliber is an
extraordinary tool in the hands of all the Esthers and Ruths
that are desperately in need of true spiritual mentors. Dr.
Halene understands first-hand how to take hold of destiny and
not let destiny go until destiny is identified.

I'm proud to call this phenomenal woman of God my
spiritual daughter of 30 years. She's a Leading Lady that does
nothing halfway. So, make some space on your calendar and
get ready to *Ignite The Leading Lady In You*. Believe me, you
will never be the same again!

Pastor Valerie Ivy Holcomb
Christian House of Prayer, Copperas Cove and Killeen, TX
Covenant Connections International (CCI)

Acknowledgements

I'm so delighted to have this opportunity to say, "Thank you!" First of all, to my Heavenly Father, Who has, I believe, led and directed me, with the help of the Holy Spirit, through the pages of this written work. I am humbled by His guidance and loving grace. I know it may sound "cliche," but without Him, I am without hope. My life is in His Hands. I'm so thankful for His lovingkindness towards me every day! I love You, my Lord and Savior Jesus Christ, but most importantly, I know You love me, and for that I'm grateful!

To my beloved husband Bishop Giddens, Jesse: you have been my motivator, mentor, model, main squeeze, and most especially, my holy man of God. You, my love, are the total package. For over 34 years, through all of life's ups and downs, you've been right there holding us both up with whatever you needed to do to "make it happen." You've always laid down your life for me. You went into the military for the sole purpose of taking care of me, Brittney, and soon after, Jonathan. I pray our marriage, with the Holy Spirit's help, continues to reflect a picture of Christ and His church (Ephesians 5:25-29). I've enjoyed our adventures in faith together, and I look forward to the future God has for us both. Thank you for giving me the space and the place to spread my wings. I love you forever and always!

To Brittney Halene-Marie and Jonathan David: I love you both so very much. I'm grateful to God every day to be your mom. I pray your hopes and dreams do come true.

To my loving parents, Pearline and the late Edwin Chamberlayne: although dad has gone on to be with the Lord, I just wanted to take this opportunity to let you know, Mom, I'm so appreciative of you both and for your unconditional love for me. I know your abundant, overflowing love has been the stabilizing force that has kept me grounded through my life's journey. Thank you for your continued support for every single thing I do.

To my mother and father in the faith, Pastor Valerie Ivy Holcomb and the late Apostle Nathaniel Holcomb: I thank my God every day for allowing my husband, children, and me to be members of the Christian House of Prayer in Copperas Cove and Killeen, Texas, and also a part of Covenant Connections International (CCI). What an amazing experience of hearing and receiving the unadulterated Word of God every time we stepped foot in the House of God. God kissed us from Heaven by giving us both of you as our spiritual parents. The deposit of the Word of God has been life-changing. The faith walk you have both lived and continue to live, Pastor Val, behind the pulpit and outside of it, has been a beautiful depiction of God's amazing grace. Thank you so much for allowing us to see what holy living looks like. We have been changed forever. Our Heavenly Father gave us the absolute best when He gave us the both of you as our pastors and spiritual leaders.

To my Good Good Girlfriends (GGGF): you said I could, and I did! Your friendship is priceless. Blessings to you, my dear friends.

To my Destiny Christian Center family and the D.I.M.A. fellowship: I love you. Thank you for loving me. As you allow the Word of God to continue to have full reign in your lives, may you prosper daily in your endeavor to fulfill your divine call to destiny, now and in the days to come.

To my mother-in-love, Tawanna, and sister Jetaun: your faith journey is beautiful to behold. The appreciation and love of family are some of the true validations of one's ministry. I pray God's love continues to compel you to draw closer to Him in fellowship and a deeper covenant relationship. I love you very much.

To the amazing Leading Ladies of Destiny Christian Center: your continued relentless effort to support me is humbling as well as uplifting. May you, beautiful ladies, be *Excessively Blessed* in every area of your lives!

To every lovely lady who will pick up this book: be inspired to take the lead! It's already in you to do so; it won't be difficult. Sometimes, all it takes is a little spark to become ignited!

Igniting The Leading Lady In You

Just A Note...

"If you don't like to read,
you haven't found the right book."
J. K. ROWLING

I love books. I like to collect, read them and look at them piled on my desk; even if I don't finish them, I like the nuggets and the treasures they hold inside. One prominent theologian said, "Even if you don't like the book at the start, read a few lines of it anyway; you never know what invaluable information you may receive just from opening up a chapter or two!" Likewise, I enjoy reading stories— some romance, some history, even mystery, and suspense. The written word holds so much more meaning and depth than what can be expressed on the screen.

Books can hold powerful truths and insights for our betterment; good stories can keep our attention from beginning to end with exciting plots and twists and lead us into events with perfectly placed dialogue and exciting drama. Some books build our interests and lead us to an ultimate conclusion for midterm correction or a new direction. Other books make us think and say, "Ok, I can implement some of these things! I can do this!" I love these kinds of books!

Most, if not all, good reads have one thought, theme, or common thread that carries you from one development to another. This isn't that type of book: I have a few thoughts, and I didn't want to cater to one group of people who may pick this book up and peruse through it! Instead, I have several thoughts I wanted to share, and through it, I hope that you would be inspired, blessed, and even changed by the inspiration and help of the Holy Spirit.

I pray that as you read through the pages, at least one thing will touch your heart and illuminate your mind; if that's the case, then I've done my job. If you receive more than one thing, that'll be great, and if you enjoy the entire book, coming away a little better than before, then that's an A+ for me! Thank you for choosing to read it. I hope you enjoy it; if not, just read a couple of chapters and pause. Come back to it and try again later! Now, let's get to it!

ANOTHER NOTE...

Can you believe it? We're in a pandemic! Wow, what in the world? Who would have thought such a thing was even possible during our lifetime? Well, if you'd like to listen to the scientists, they made some predictions concerning this very thing. Although there is no perfect science, that's why they call it predictions. Sometimes, we may just need to pay attention. It's not about whether we listen to God or science. God and science are not pitted against each other. Our God created everything; so when you study science, nature, or the trends that produce the study of science, it's all Him. Even if people in our society try to leave Him out, it isn't possible. His signature is on it all!

ANYWAY...

My hope is that by the time this book is released we are, to some degree, on the better side of this life-altering circumstance and situation! It is also my hope that at some point in this moment, we've taken the time to help another individual or several individuals with either prayer, acts of service, or simply being kind and compassionate toward one another. That's how we manage and maneuver through a crisis, especially a worldwide pandemic!

Kindness and love never grow old. We become the better and the richer for it—emotionally, mentally, and spiritually—because we extend freely without looking for its reward. It's one of the best ways to make friends and influence people (hopefully, that thought puts a smile on your face).

This pandemic has caused us, to a degree, to see some things differently, hopefully for the better. We may have also learned to do some things differently, hopefully for the better! Either way, it doesn't matter what's in the way; with help from our Heavenly Father, we can make a way and eventually do it a better way! Our personal mantra, as well as our ministry mantra, has continued to be, "Do it anyway, just do it a different way!"

With every trial, test, and pop-up problem we face, they

should change us for the betterment of ourselves and others, especially those in our present scope of influence. That's my prayer; that's my heartfelt desire; that's my hope!

If you're reading this book, you've made it! Right here in this very moment, you're here, right here. So, what are you going to do with the rest of your life, or if that's too heavy to ponder, perhaps just the rest of your day? Either way, you've made it to another day; you can make it through every day because you can do anything a different way!

Whatever your plans are, even if you haven't made specific plans for the present or future, perhaps this book will give you a little boost to, as my son Jonathan likes to say, "Make some things happen!" Planning is a good thing, keeping in mind this one specific thing:

You can make many plans,
but the LORD's purpose will prevail.
Proverbs 19:21 (NLT)

Whether you're a Leading Lady who is a believer or not, what you want is the Lord's purpose for your life to prevail! *Prevail*, in its simplest definition, means *to come out on top*! And if the Lord has His say and His way in and over your life, then prevailing is just what you'll do!

AN INVITATION...

Leading Lady, I hope above all that you — yes, I mean

18

you—would prosper and endeavor to be ***excessively blessed*** in every area of your life.

Leading Lady, if you would like to receive the Lord Jesus as your personal Lord and Savior, you can take the time to do so right now. Simply say these words:

"Lord Jesus, come into my heart.
Forgive me, heal me, and change me from the inside out.
I love you, and I need You. Thank You for receiving me!"

Preface

"Today a reader, tomorrow a leader."
MARGARET FULLER

I'm so excited for you, Leading Lady of God's Heart, to read this book, *Igniting The Leading Lady In You*! Although I broach several topics like marriage, money, ministry, keeping your mind, and everything in between, this book has one common thread and sole purpose. Its purpose is to encourage women — every woman — in all walks of life to recognize their full strength of potential and purpose on this side of Heaven. My goal is to encourage each precious Lady in the journey you are on in this life. I want to boost your endurance to keep pressing forward!

The prevailing thought and theme, if you would, is that no matter what you've experienced in your life, sweet woman of God, you have been set aside, anointed in fact, for God's great purpose for you! Therefore, no matter what's going on around you or even if there's turmoil inside you, you are seen, you are heard, you are loved, and you matter to your Heavenly Father.

I really want you to know that your Heavenly Father has His eyes on you (Deuteronomy 32:8)! You are the center of His attention, and He has great things in store for your life—yep, for your everyday living experience!

Oh, and by the way, you'll see plenty of scripture references without the verses. You can take your time to go into the Word and read them in the King James Version or a couple of different translations if you like! That's what makes studying the Word of God pretty cool! I also add scriptures with verses in several translations to bring some clarity to the thoughts that are shared! So, all in all, it should be a pretty well-rounded read for your enjoyment. At least that's my desire!

God has placed His Hand on us to lead in life together— yes, together and not by ourselves. Each of us has a gift of grace and a goal to accomplish on this side of life. With the help of God, I want to encourage you to go after it! God has called you, and God is still calling you even if you haven't answered Him yet. If you haven't quite heard His Voice compelling you to what's next or answered Him up to this point, don't worry; you can pick up right now, right where you are, and hear what the Lord has laid out just for you!

Are you excited yet?

I hope as you open the pages of this book that you would indeed be ignited in your heart and mind to do you! I am talking about the you that's set aside for the Glory of God to be the very best you that you can possibly be! That's the goal, and that's the gain. You'll never be satisfied until you fulfill your God-given, God-designed, God-inspired purpose on this side of life! It's already in you to succeed and to win; you're prewired to do well. You have all the makings of greatness in your life. You've just got to tap into the well of God's goodness that He wants to pour out on you for success! Oh boy! Ok, I'm excited for you to delve into the pages of this printed work!

So, that's it! That's what this writing is all about. It's about getting you stirred up and keeping you stirred up to do what only you have been created to do. That's what we're going to discuss throughout the chapters in this book. We'll look into the Word of God at the lives, traumas, dramas, victories, and deliverances of matriarchs and some patriarchs.

I'll give you a couple of adventure stories and anecdotes about myself and some of the experiences I've had in the hopes of getting you going if you haven't done so already. We'll talk a bit about other inspiring Leading Ladies—icons who were courageous in their time, extraordinary women from our past, and those here with us presently. There'll also be some great quotes sprinkled throughout the pages that I hope you enjoy.

If you have already started fulfilling your purpose, then hopefully, through the help of God's Holy Spirit, we can squeeze out the more that's in you! Oh, you didn't know?! You've got more to give and more to get! So, let's get into it! By the way, I just want you to know that age is not a barrier to you walking, even right now, into the best part of your life!

I watched an interview on a late-night tv show one evening, and the topic of discussion sparked me. The host spoke with a news anchor about a special interest piece she had been working on. The presentation was about women in their 50s, 60s, 70s and on into their 80s discovering and fulfilling what they believed was their lifelong purpose! I was so enthused by her speaking about these distinctly different women doing their thing in their latter years! She described how elated and driven these women were who'd found great success in their purpose later in life! She said they were invigorated by all that they were able to do!

I'm telling you there's more in you! We just need to tap into it! And that's really what this entire compilation is all about! So, I really do hope through reading this book that you get excited and ignited to be the very best you that our great God has destined you to be!

This book is ultra-positive, no negative stuff here! There's only good stuff in this book to feast on! This assortment of thoughts, narratives, and stories is not designed to make you feel uncomfortable or bad about what you may or may not be doing. It's only meant to charge you up about what you can be doing! You may have seen, heard, or read things before this book, but here it is again! There's greatness inside of you, and that's what we want to tap into, to pull it right up and out of you!

Why? Why do we want to pull out the greatness in you? It's simple and for the following reason: as my husband, Bishop Jesse Giddens, and our father in the faith, Apostle Holcomb used to teach, it's for your growth, God's Glory, and others' gain. You are here on this planet for a very special reason, and no matter how big or small you think it is, you're here to fulfill it! Most likely, you may already be doing it—at least part of it!

Dr. Halene Giddens

Just embrace it wholeheartedly, appreciate it abundantly, and do more! It's all there, right there in you to do!

Ok! Now, are you ready to get started? Alright! Go ahead turn the page!

Igniting The Leading Lady In You

Dr. Halene Giddens

God is within her,

she will not fall;

God will help her

at break of day.

Psalm 46:5 (NIV)

Igniting The Leading Lady In You

CHAPTER 1

Do You Know Who You Are?

"In order to get the right idea of ourselves, we first need to figure out who we really are."
DR. PREM JAGYASI

Knowing who you are, as I'm sure we can all attest to, can sometimes be quite confusing. Our roles in our everyday functional activity can tend to define us. Maybe you're a wife and/or mother, perhaps you're single looking to be married or not, or a divorcee looking forward to single-hood or not. You may be a widow grappling with what to do with the rest of your life and how this different nuance defines who you are. It's not always an easy concept to figure out just who we are!

We can assuredly be defined in our thoughts and the minds of people around us by our social status, status quo, or employment situation. Some examples that I know are nurses, teachers, business owners, administrators, social workers, correctional officers, and sales personnel. Maybe you work in maintenance, landscaping, or work for your family business; you may be a domestic engineer (which, at times, can feel like constant, never-ending labor). Possibly, you are a french fry technician at the local fast-food establishment. Perhaps you're in between jobs or career choices, which tend to define us as well.

Make a careful exploration of who you are and the work you have been given, and then sink yourself into that. Don't be impressed with yourself. Don't compare yourself with others. Each of you must take responsibility for doing the creative best you can with your own life.
Galatians 6:4-5 (MSG)

IT'S NEVER TOO LATE TO BE
WHAT YOU MIGHT HAVE BEEN

This subtitle is a quote from 1800 English novelist Mary Ann Evans, who went by the pen name George Eliot. She used the name of a man so she would be taken seriously as a writer. She was a well-renowned novelist, journalist, poet, translator, and became one of the leading writers of the Victorian Era. We *can* become what we might have been; it's not too late! Isn't it amazing what we can accomplish when we set our hearts and minds to the task?

I like to try to stay hydrated by drinking plenty of water. By the way, parenthetically speaking, we should all drink water pretty regularly. Did you know that over half of our body weight is made up of water? That's quite a bit! One of the many water brands I consume is Perfect Hydration; these are the words written on the bottle: "Do you think we are all created for a purpose?" Then it reads, "I know I was; that's why I'm so much more than just water. I'm supercharged water!"

Can you imagine this particular bottle of water knowing why it was created, knowing its purpose?! Not only does it know its purpose, but it even boasts about it as well! The bottle packaging goes on to describe all that it has in it to make it the perfect water to hydrate oneself, and I do! I get excited about drinking this brand of water because I really think I'm doing something special for myself! I'm actually convinced of it! Now, I know that this is all marketing and strategy to sell their *professionally packaged product*, but it still hit me. If bottled water knows its purpose, how much more should we know ours!

> *"It takes courage to grow up*
> *and become who you really are."*
> E.E. CUMMINGS

We can allow so many things to define us, such as where we grew up and how we grew up, the pigment of our outer derma (our skin color), or the things that have happened to us over our life span. Even the experiences that shape our minds can mold our thinking of who we are. Our thoughts of who we are can be manipulated, especially by the people with whom we interact. The people, things, and situations that we allow to influence our lives help shape our opinions about ourselves. Significant moments can leave impressions in our hearts, souls, and psyche. These experiences, situations, and people can drastically formulate the course of our future for the good or the bad, and may just define who we think we are.

Of which I became a minister according to
the gift of the grace of God given to me
by the effective working of His power.
Ephesians 3:7 (NKJV)

This is my life work: helping people understand and
respond to this Message. It came as a sheer gift to me, a
real surprise, God handling all the details.
Ephesians 3:7 (MSG)

Yes, I used two different Bible translations for the same verse to emphasize the point: I am a gift, and so are you. Not only has God created a gift for you to carry, but He's also created you to be a gift! *YOU! ARE! A! GIFT!* Don't look at your outer wrapping. That's just the pretty paper presentation that the gift you and I are wrapped up in. You may say, "I don't like the packaging." Well, there are too many elixirs, serums, lotions, perfumes, cosmetics, Botox, plumpers, rollerballs, procedures, and other things that can smooth things out, tuck things in, and move things around to make the outer package pretty and to your liking.

Then there's the gym, the park, a sidewalk to walk on,

and workout regimens that you can purchase or pull up on YouTube using your electronic devices that most of us, if not all of us, carry around every day. In addition, we can probably custom make many diet plans for our hectic lives to fit into our schedules that can change any and every outer appearance that we can imagine and come up with!

What I'm talking about is the inner you; that's where the true gift lies. The gift that God has created you to be may be lying dormant inside of you. Maybe your gift comes out in little spurts every once in a while. Perhaps you're operating right in your gift and you haven't actually realized it, or maybe you have tapped right into the gift of who you are! You'll know it because it's your happy place. It's the place that makes you feel like you're right in the pocket of what you're meant to do and who you're meant to be. It's you in operation with the gift of God flowing through you.

My dear brothers and sisters, don't be fooled. Every good present and every perfect gift comes from above, from the Father who made the sun, moon, and stars. The Father doesn't change like the shifting shadows produced by the sun and the moon. God decided to give us life through the word of truth to make us his most important creatures.
James 1:16-18 (GWT)

Yep, God has made each one of us a gift! Now, I know that none of us are perfect. Yup, that's right. We are not perfect. If you think you are perfect or even slightly close to perfection, that's a problem called narcissism. That's something we would need to most definitely deal with—perhaps in another book. I digress. Let me move on. The gift of who you are is to be used for the benefit of others. You, as a gift, can be cultivated and refined by use and with training.

YOU ARE THE GIFT

On the package of my Red Vines licorice, there was a quote, which read, "It takes only a moment for the giver to perform an act of kindness, but it takes a lifetime for the receiver to forget it." Isn't it amazing that being the gift you are can drastically change the life of someone you encounter! That's why the gift of who you are should be used intentionally! So, every morning when you get up, get ready, and walk out of the door, you should yell out, "I'm a gift to the world!" Ok, maybe you shouldn't yell outside your front door, but at least tell yourself, "I've been made to be a gift for at least someone or many someone's today!"

Another quote I like says, "Your talent is God's gift to you, but what you do with it is your gift back to God." God has made you a gift to others for their benefit first and then for yours. As a result, you get the blessings and the benefits of being a gift to others around you and even away from you, depending on how far your gift reaches! God has created you as a gift, a working gift given out to others in your sphere and even sometimes outside it.

But God was kind! He made me what I am, and his wonderful kindness wasn't wasted. I worked much

harder than any of the other apostles, although it was
really God's kindness at work and not me.
1 Corinthians 15:10 (CEV)

Apostle Holcomb used to say, "Our identity is found in Christ's Divinity." Simply put, who we are is found in Him, Jesus Christ, our Lord and Savior! That just makes good sense, doesn't it? Our Creator knows exactly what He created. He knows my purpose, He handcrafted me for it, and He certainly knows and has handcrafted yours as well! The more I submit and commit my life to Him, the more I come to know and accept who I am, the gifting I have, and the talents that are naturally on the inside of me.

God created us, formed us, and fashioned us to have His qualities and attributes by His Divine Design. I know this seems mind-boggling and even daunting; instead, it should give us great peace! We have the likeness of God, our Creator, working on the inside of us. This God, our Father, Who loves us like absolutely no one else can and no one else ever will, hand-picked us for His Purpose! He knows exactly who you are right now and what He's destined you to become. It's not even plausible to completely comprehend the manifold love of God towards each one of us! He loves you, He loves me, and that's incredible to internalize! This love that our Heavenly Father has for us is meant to enrich our lives in every facet of life for this reason: to fulfill and fully figure out who we are!

The whole reason we are here on planet earth is that this Holy, Heavenly God has all this love to express, and He, first of all, expresses that love to us and then expresses it through us. His love pours into every nook and cranny of our being, leaving no area unfulfilled. His love for us is so amazing and complete in every way that our vocabulary isn't vast enough to fully explain the astounding, all-consuming, overflowing, never-ending, always giving, ever abounding, exceptionally perfect love of God! This is how we live our fantastic, fulfilling life of love for our God, knowing who we are and who He's created us to be.

Indeed, who we are is wrapped up in Who He is! Therefore, the created gift that He made out of you has been fashioned, designed, and tailor-made just for you. That simply means only *you* can precisely do what He created *you* to do. No one else can fit into this perfect mold God formulated for you. Now, if you decide never to walk in who you are and do what He's given you to do, someone else could fulfill some aspect of it but not the way you can! Only *you* can do what only *you* can do. God had you in mind when He graced you with the gift you carry around on the inside of you. You might want to ponder this for just a moment.

With that being said, He divested Himself in each one of us! And we have His spiritual DNA working inside of us! That's a big wow! Our Heavenly Father is a Creative Being, and He can't help but create; that's why He's called The Creator! This is what's working inside of you: a creative flow that needs to be developed, worked on, and then released outside of you! This is not to be overwhelming, but instead, it should be comforting, securing, and even settling to each of us who may be seeking and searching for who we are.

---

*God spoke: "Let us make human beings in our image,
make them reflecting our nature. So they can be
responsible for the fish in the sea, the birds in the air,
the cattle, And, yes, Earth itself, and every animal
that moves on the face of Earth." God created human
beings; he created them godlike, Reflecting God's nature.
He created them male and female. God blessed them:
"Prosper! Reproduce! Fill Earth! Take charge! Be
responsible for fish in the sea and birds in the air, for
every living thing that moves on the face of Earth."*
Genesis 1:26-28 (MSG)

*God looked over everything he had made; it was so good,
so very good! It was evening, it was morning
—Day Six.*
Genesis 1:31 (MSG)

Wow, this is fantastic news! God in His Holy Habitation looked at what He made and said not only is it "so good," but it is "so very good!" We have been created to prosper, reproduce and fill the earth! We can do well and prosper on this side of life. This is part of the tools He's given us to accomplish, an abundant life that overflows with God's Goodness and Grace!

---

*But remember the LORD your God, for it is he who
gives you the ability to produce wealth...*
Deuteronomy 8:18 (NIV)

THE GIFT TO PROFIT

Prosperity is not a negative word. The ability to obtain wealth is given by God in His Perfect Will for each of us to receive and share! The prosperity you accumulate may be the catalyst God uses to move your purpose and His Plan for your life forward. Your prosperity may also be used to help finance the purpose of others. Either way, it's not just for you to be rich, but to reach out to organizations and people for great causes! Some have the gift to generate finances for the purpose of sowing and giving. That's what they do! That is their gift!

If God has given us this opportunity to prosper, we've got to find out first how to do it with what we're working with right now. Then once we've worked that out with God's Help, we need to discover what to do properly with the finances we continually receive. Oh, He has a plan for you to handle what you have been given with wisdom! Your money is a part of His Perfect Plan for you as well. Though it's not the entire plan, it is still a part of it. Therefore, we need to learn how to have, handle, and hold our finances for the benefit of ourselves and the betterment of others.

Good people leave an inheritance to their grandchildren,
but the sinner's wealth passes to the godly.
Proverbs 13:22 (NLT)

It's ok, Leading Ladies, to talk about your money, and if God said you're supposed to have it, you need to be able to handle it as well. This is not just for the men in the house because there are plenty of wealthy women. These ladies know how to generate financial prosperity, and they know how to work with it.

Let me reiterate this point: God wants you to be blessed in every way! You can learn how to work with what you're working with as well! I'm talking about your money right here, and if you can't handle it, getting the help you need is necessary for your future. We all have hardships that hit our lives in so many ways, but we must remain focused on our Heavenly Father to help us when the troubles hit.

Beloved, I pray that in every way you may succeed and prosper and be in good health [physically], just as [I know] your soul prospers [spiritually].
3 John 1:2 (AMP)

THE GIFT OF REPRODUCTION AND DOMINION

You may think I've veered off track, but this is all attached to the making of who you are! When we look back over Genesis, also known as the Book of Beginnings, God's Word says in the Message Translation we are to prosper, reproduce, fill the earth, and take charge. By the way, to reproduce and fill the earth doesn't mean just having children. It also means to reproduce the person you've become by experience, the good things in you, and the gift God placed in you. Reproduce the kind of person you are meant to be, filling the earth by reaching out to others in wonderful ways and bringing positive change, whether great or small! Yes, you can do this and produce gradual and greater value to others around you!

Furthermore, you are meant to ***take charge***! People in this world have taken this philosophy and have twisted it to mean something hideous. We were never to have "dominion," as the King James Version words it, over other human beings. We were to have dominion over every living thing in the earth, but NOT over each other—not even a husband over his wife, especially not that! God did not give a wife to a man for him to dominate or subdue! Neither is a husband given to a wife to rule over in any way, shape, or form! This has been our destruction and downfall.

But thanks be to God, even though we dominate one another with all this twisted and wrong behavior in our thinking, God continues to show us His Mercy and Love. Because of His Kindness, we can still succeed, prosper, produce, reproduce, fill the earth and even take charge the right way! Nope, Ladies, I didn't say charge it! I said, Take Charge! Take charge of what? Our personal life, our future, our right now, and every moment in between!

Now, taking charge doesn't mean you don't listen to those around you, especially to the people who have gone before you and those who have your best interest at heart. Taking charge means you're setting your goals and mapping out the road designed to get you there! You aren't simply letting things happen to you, but you're making things happen for you! Yes, you may need some help with this process, and there's absolutely nothing wrong with that! Get it! Get what you need to succeed!

You should say right here and right now, "I'm about to take charge over myself and my life, over my mind and my emotions, and over everything that concerns me! I'm taking charge!" Why do you even have the authority to speak this boldly? Because God has commanded you and me to take charge! You just read it in His Word! The best way and the only way to *take charge* is to know who you are and why you are here.

THE GIFT OF PURPOSE

There is absolutely a reason for your existence. You, my lovely lady, are not a mistake! I drank from another bottle of water with these words written on them, "I am not trash," and neither are you and me! You are neither a waste, nor a waste of time! I don't care how you came to be where you are at this moment. You are here for *PURPOSE*! And if anyone said otherwise, then they have lied to you. I repeat: they *lied to you*!

"Before I shaped you in the womb,
I knew all about you. Before you saw the light of day,
I had holy plans for you: A prophet to the nations —
that's what I had in mind for you."
Jeremiah 1:5 (MSG)

In the above scripture, we understand that God is speaking directly to the prophet Jeremiah. God was convincing him of the ministry He'd called Jeremiah into. Now, God is speaking directly to you! There is a plan and a place for you and me as well. God knows each one of us by name. Matthew 10:30 shows us that He has even numbered the hairs on our heads, and He knew us before we were even a thought in the minds of our parents!

Before we were in the womb of our mothers, our Heavenly Father was looking forward to the day we arrived on this side of life! He said, "Oh, here she comes, and I can't wait until she looks my way, so I can take her on this journey called life! It's not always going to be easy, but I'll be with her every step of the way (Hebrews 13:5)!" God promises us that He'll always be with us through the good, the bad, and the ugly times of our lives, and in and through it all, we are to realize what we're doing here!

"You weren't an accident. You weren't mass-produced. You aren't an assembly-line product. You were deliberately planned, specifically gifted, and lovingly positioned on the earth by the Master Craftsman."
MAX LUCADO

I sure hope you read that quote again, even if you think you already know it because reading it more than once helps to solidify the point. So, read it again and again and replace the words "you weren't" to "I'm not" and then "you were" to "I am!"

If you haven't gotten the message yet, discovering who you **really** are takes giving your God-given life back to the Giver of life.

*"Salvation through Jesus Christ – this is the
ultimate message of the Bible, and the core of Christianity.
Other religions have great leaders and noble principles,
but Christianity is different because our God died to save us
and then rose to give us eternal life!"*
PASTOR JACK WELLMAN

After the saving part of God's Purpose comes the gift of
God's Work through us!

---

*Saving is all his idea, and all his work. All we do is
trust him enough to let him do it. It's God's gift from
start to finish! We don't play the major role.
If we did, we'd probably go around bragging that we'd
done the whole thing! No, we neither make nor save
ourselves. God does both the making and saving.
He creates each of us by Christ Jesus to join him in the
work he does, the good work he has gotten ready for us to
do, work we had better be doing.*
Ephesians 2:8-10 (MSG)

CREATION'S GIFT

This "work" the scripture in Ephesians talks about is what
we've been created by our Heavenly Father to do. Like the
scripture says, it was God's idea in the first place! He created
you; He made you; He graced you; and He gifted you. I want
you to literally say, "I'm gifted by God." Yes, God graced
every person to be a gift. Finding out the gift you are takes

discovering your talent and spending time with your Creator to find out why you were created!

> *"Make the most of yourself,*
> *for that is all there is of you."*
> RALPH WALDO EMERSON

I know that sounds kind of funny, but we should indeed "Be the best me that me can be!" I know that's a bit of Ebonics, but it flows well, and I think we can remember it well! Because as you have seen, heard, and I'm sure have read many times, no one can beat you at being you. At this moment, you are reading this line so you can become all that you were created to be! I just can't say it enough! Be all that God created you to be! It doesn't matter how minuscule you may think it is or how small you think you are; you have been commissioned, set aside, and set apart to be all that, and, yes, a bag of chips! I wanted to start this book with you getting pumped about being more of you. The you you're supposed to be!

> *The LORD our God has blessed us, and so now there*
> *are as many of us as there are stars in the sky. God has*
> *even promised to bless us a thousand times more,*
> *and I pray that he will.*
> Deuteronomy 1:10-11 (CEV)

We understand in the above scripture that Moses is speaking to the children of Israel to become stronger by increasing in number. Yet, my prayer for you is that you would increase in your confidence in God and personally become more of who He has created you to be! As you continue to get to know God more and begin to know yourself, an increase is inevitable!

I pray the same as well: may you be blessed a thousand times more in your finances! May you be blessed a thousand times more in your capacity to receive and hear from the Lord. And may you be blessed a thousand times more in the pursuit of your purpose as you always allow our God to be your Guide!

But you are a chosen generation, a royal priesthood, a holy nation, His own special people, that you may proclaim the praises of Him who called you out of darkness into His marvelous light; who once were not a people but are now the people of God, who had not obtained mercy but now have obtained mercy.
I Peter 2:9-10 (NKJV)

You, my dear friend, are chosen, and you have been chosen to do better and to be better. You are royal, and you are holy because you are His! You have been given the assignment to discover who you are. And you will find that out as you trust and believe what God's Word says about you! You have been set aside as special, and you have a specialized gift stirring inside of you.

Each person has been handcrafted by God and has a grace gifting in them. I want to go on to the next chapter, leaving you with these quotes to accelerate you into forward motion and encourage you to discover who you really are!

*"Be the kind of Woman
other women like to be around."*
ANONYMOUS

*"Be the kind of woman that both your 11 year old self
and your 90 year old self would be proud of."*
RACHEL HOLLIS

*"You are more than you ever expected
and better than you imagined!"*
ANONYMOUS

I'm not sure when and where I read the last quote, but it made me think about every beautiful person that would pick up this book and get to this quote. So, since you're reading this right now, I thought of you! Go ahead, read it again. Read it at least three more times so that the truth of these words will sit right in your heart and mind and stay there.

*"You are more than you ever expected
and better than you imagined!"*
ANONYMOUS

These last couple of quotes have also inspired me.

*"Be the kind of woman who understands
that in big and small ways,
she is capable of doing amazing things in this world."*
ANONYMOUS

Dr. Halene Giddens

"Be the kind of woman that fixes another woman's crown without telling the world that it was crooked."
LESLIE LITTLEJOHN

I leave you with this one:

FROM YOURS TRULY...

Be the kind of woman who knows who she is, all because who she is is centered in Who He is and knowing Him, her Creator!

Igniting The Leading Lady In You

CHAPTER 2

Blood Diamond

"I like pressure.
Diamonds are made under pressure,
and I definitely enjoy it."
CAROLINE BUCHANAN

I n 2006, *Blood Diamond*, starring Leonardo DiCaprio and Djimon Hounsou, came to the big screen. This movie depicts the horrors that surrounded the diamond trade to countries worldwide to finance the civil wars in Sierra Leone back in 1991- 2002. Sierra Leone is on the southwest coast of West Africa, bordered by Liberia to its southeast and Guinea to its northeast.

This motion picture is a biting portrayal that explores the atrocities of war for profit, which still takes place today. *Blood Diamond* was written to expose the ill-conceived schemes to acquire diamonds, one of the many priceless natural resources found in this war-torn country. This movie also portrays the many lives lost simply due to greed and the desire for power and money. Although a fictional story, it is based on documented events that took place for many years up to this point throughout the country.

The love of power, money, and recognition is so prevalent in our society as a whole. It can become the driving force behind almost every action taken. It becomes the entire purpose for which some people live! Therefore, the Word of God warns us against this behavior and thought process as believers.

Don't love the world's ways. Don't love the world's goods. Love of the world squeezes out love for the Father. Practically everything that goes on in the world — wanting your own way, wanting everything for yourself, wanting to appear important — has nothing to do with the Father. It just isolates you from him.
1 John 2:15-16 (MSG)

These are engaging to the world and can be detrimental to others and ourselves: prestige, power, prominence, and prosperity. As believers in Christ, we are part of this world and this world's system, meaning we have to operate in it. We all have the same frailty to be drawn away and enticed at any given moment (James 1:14).

Now, you may say in your mind that you have no desire to

acquire success and wealth at the cost of your spiritual health in God. Perhaps in your heart of hearts, these pursuits have never been the driving force behind your motivations to obtain the things that make you happy or the purposes that draw you. However, the appeal of success of any kind is always attractive. We must protect ourselves from being taken in by even the slightest lure of the world's concept of achieving success.

Success in marriage, ministry, mainstream society, and the making of money are motivators that people strive for. Having the desire and opportunity to "make it" in this life is essential for most individuals. Goals and dreams are never wrong pursuits. Going after things, positions, or positive directions you believe in is not wrong either. It's "the way" in which we seek to go after these things. Even if they are Godly aims and purposes, we can get off and go off track. The "thing," whether it be the ministry, the business, or the title, can become our sole purpose, not necessarily "the way" in achieving it. Thus, you should always be careful of "the way" to get the "thing."

That's not to say God doesn't have good success for us. He most certainly does, according to Joshua 1:8! However, we must understand that all success isn't good success! We cannot look at the world's success as the measure of what good success looks like. Neither can we always look at the outward appearance of a person, place, or thing's success as a measuring factor for our own success story. The most important thing in pursuing our happiness and gaining our goals is that we should always consult our Heavenly Father's Direction and receive His Correction. Good success is always found in seeking Him first in everything we do.

---

*What I'm trying to do here is to get you to relax,
to not be so preoccupied with getting, so you can respond
to God's giving. People who don't know God and
the way he works fuss over these things,
but you know both God and how he works.
Steep your life in God-reality, God-initiative,
God-provisions. Don't worry about missing out. You'll
find all your everyday human concerns will be met.*
Matthew 6:31-33 (MSG)

What's so amazing is God's priority to give. That's what He desires to do for each one of us! He gave His Only Begotten Son, Jesus Christ, to be crucified on the Cross so that we could have an open-ended relationship with Him! He gave the earth and everything in it for us to live, thrive, and receive it with thanksgiving (2 Corinthians 9:10-11).

The precious gems continually mined in these countries in Africa were easily accessible to the first settlers in the land (Genesis 2:10-12). God never intended for these gems to motivate greed in people all over the world. If humankind were not so into greed, there would be enough to go around for anyone who desired to delight in these precious jewels! I believe this because we serve a Generously Giving God, and He gives us all things richly to enjoy (1 Timothy 6:17)! He is the God of Love, Generosity, and Abundance (Ephesians 3:20; 2 Corinthians 9:8).

Giving has always been God's idea. Receiving has always

been His intention for us, but it always must start with giving. Giving leads to receiving, and this includes God giving the land the nutrients it needs to produce the natural resources. This has always been the way of God. Living organisms produce and reproduce life like we do. Like other living organism, the soil needs nutrients to regenerate and procreate. If the soil doesn't receive what it needs, it cannot bring forth the quantity or the quality of what it's been created to produce (Leviticus 25:2-6). That's why all living things need times of rest so that they can recover in order to replenish (Genesis 2:2,3; Acts 3:19).

To continue to blossom, bloom, and grow, you must receive the nutrients you need every day that comes from spending time with the Giver of Life, our Heavenly Father, Who is our God (Hosea 10:12). Natural nutrients and spiritual nutrients are required to live a fruitful life. We need both to continue to survive and thrive. After receiving Him into your heart, God's great hope for you is to be and do everything that you have been placed in position to be and do on this earth. To produce the good fruits God has already begun to stir in your heart requires staying connected to the Vine. Jesus Christ is the Vine of Life from which we receive all of our nutrients (John 15:5,6). When we stay connected to Jesus, we have all we need, all the good things working in us to bear that sweet fruit that our world needs to receive from us (Romans 8:19; Philippians 1:6,10,11).

"Nothing good will come from you
if there's not something good happening
on the inside of you."
BRIAN BRANAM

That may seem a bit harsh, but so truly stated. We must intentionally take care of our inner self. Get this: it's even more important than the outer self (1 Timothy 4:8)! Those beautiful mountains in Africa hold some of the most exquisite and exceptional jewels on the inside of them, and it takes extreme hard labor and work to retrieve them. As I said, I don't believe that was always the case. I believe these jewels were on display for everyone to see. I believe they glistened with their glory! I believe people from near and far could see those shimmering, sparkling, exuberant, precious stones from miles around. All things were in perfect balance in giving and receiving. The mountains received the highest level of nutrients from the sun, the water, and the animals that inhabited the land. Everything worked together to produce those beautiful gems found up high in those mountains nestled in the deep soil within the earth!

When good things are happening inside you, you can't help but for good things to come out of you and to be seen and experienced by those who come in contact with you! That's why you've got to make sure you're always putting good stuff in you like the Word of God, positive affirming words, and surrounding yourself with positive people that will speak into your purpose! But, be aware of people who continually zap you of your strength by drawing all the good things out of you and never filling and fueling you to be able to move forward towards your future efforts!

Even when negative things are spoken to you and about you or when awful and evil things happen around you or to you, keep speaking up and speaking out with powerful positive words that produce healing and hope in you, for you, and then in others around you! The help you give to others—those who truly appreciate you—helps you develop and grow! It can also help you heal from wounds you've received from your past experiences! It activates your inner resources and causes you to produce more and more!

Your outer circumstances don't have to determine your inner peace. God can and will use the outer and inner circumstances to work for your good (Romans 8:28; 2 Corinthians 9:8). That's where peace comes in, knowing it's all going to work for you, and it's all going to work out for you! The sun, the rain, and the mess the animals leave behind all work together for you to become the precious jewel God intended for you to be!

RAW MATERIAL

When we look at all of the many jewels produced out of the mines in the nation of Africa, we see God's Handy Work in play. The process used by the elements—the harshness of the weather and the extreme exposure to nothing but deep darkness, wet, cold, and the sun's heat—all come together to make jewels, gems, gold, and other precious metals. Even the years in waiting to be discovered are all used in the production of the outcome.

Precious jewels and gems are something God gave to show a sign of importance to the wearer (Exodus 28:15-20). Those chosen and hand-picked by God to wear these sparkling gems knew that they were set aside as distinct and distinguished. Even today, when we receive a special stone to wear or purchase a high-priced one for ourselves, we appreciate the value of the jewels. We enjoy their beauty. The larger the stone, the more attention it receives.

In the Old Testament, when the priest of the Lord wore the breastplate of stones over his heart, each jewel represented a certain tribe. When the priests went into the Holy of Holies to pray for the children of Israel, they wore the jewels close to their hearts. This symbolized not only God's Love for them but also the position the children of Israel held in His Heart for each of them. It was a place of regard and honor, and the jewels represented God's High esteem for His people. What value He placed on them as His chosen people. Each stone was different, and no stone could be cut exactly the same. It wasn't possible to do so, which signified God's awareness of their beauty and unique qualities: all very precious, extraordinary, and important! Each one had its own sparkle and shine!

God never intended for the gems to replace you or me in significance. These jewels were always meant to reflect and represent the value and worth He places on each of us! They were just a glimmer of the glory He's made each of us to be!

> *"No one knows how precious you are.*
> *You are a diamond in the rough*
> *and with a little polishing,*
> *you will shine."*
> LOUNG UNG

You, my dear Leading Lady, are a precious jewel in the sight of God as His treasured possession and His chosen, royal, and special priest of the Lord (Malachi 3:17, Exodus 19:5, 1 Peter 2:9). In all that you've been through and experienced, don't allow the awful or hard stuff to make you bitter, but only let it make you better. That's what it's all meant to do! It's all used together for you to become a jewel. You are a jewel!

JEWEL

You are the glistening, sparkling diamond that God wants to show off, so those around you see, experience, and partake in the beauty that is you! Don't allow anyone nor anything to diminish your shine. You, my dear girl, are God's greatest accomplishment! You've got the grit to get up, get going, shimmer, and shine because, girl, you are golden! If I were preaching this point, I'd say it one more time, but since the words are written on this page, it's sealed so that you can read it again and again anytime!

When a diamond or any precious stone is cut, it reflects a new sparkle and a different shine. The shine is almost blinding in its brilliance every time the light hits it, especially when the sun is reflecting off of it! It's noticeable, and people are drawn to the sparkle. Others around you may not know what it took to get that shine. All they experience is the brilliance, the beauty, and the blessing that you are! The cuts in your life, the bad breaks, the broken pieces, and the refining were all used for your making. This is what makes you so intricately unique and perfectly fashioned to bling in the light. Your sparkle reflects the glory of the Son, not the s-u-n, rather the S-O-N! You shine bright, and you shine best when you're reflecting His Light in and through you!

Here is the final crux of the matter! This is what I especially want you, the Leading Lady of God's Heart, to know! You are the diamond our Father finds precious; you are a diamond that He has purchased with His own Blood. You are the diamond that's covered by the Blood of Jesus, and that's what makes you so incredibly special! This is the reason you are so very lovely, precious, and positively remarkable! He is the reason we can have that ever-brightening glimmer of light that can never be snuffed out!

You shall also be [so beautiful and prosperous as to be thought of as] a crown of glory and honor in the hand of the Lord, and a royal diadem [exceedingly beautiful] in the hand of your God.
Isaiah 62:3 (AMPC)

You've got to see yourself in the light of His Glory. You've got to see yourself excelling in every expectation that you have set before you!

The Greek word for *diamond* is *adamas*, meaning **unbreakable or indestructible**! It is the hardest substance found in nature. The metaphor 'shine like a diamond' has always represented 'mental toughness' and 'inner integrity.

"A diamond's creation requires immense pressure and intense temperatures to reach its highest potential. Without enduring the adversity and pressure of its environment, the diamond would never become the treasure it was meant to be."
SUSAN C. YOUNG

Every individual has the potential to be a diamond glowing with beauty and vitality on the outside while remaining sane, wise, and solid inside. So, Leading Lady, this is you: this is what our God created you to be and what you have on the inside, working on the outside of you!

"A diamond doesn't start out polished and shining. It once was nothing special, but with enough pressure and time, becomes spectacular. I'm that diamond."
SOLANGE NICOLE

You are that diamond as well! The Blood Jesus shed for you and me is most especially for our salvation. This Blood perfects you and makes you into the brilliant shine God made you to be! So, don't allow anything or anyone to diminish your sparkle or dull your glow!

"Life tries to crush her, but only succeeded in making a diamond."
JOHN GREEN

Like those precious gems dug out of the earth, they have value to the person who finds them, and a high price is placed on each stone. I hope you have a real understanding of how valuable your price is. Take stock in yourself and rise to the exceptional potential that causes you to shine brightly like the diamond you are! The Blood of the Master Creator causes it to be so! God has placed upon you your value that exceeds any sparkling gem that can be found (Proverbs 31:10). Let me express this again: you, my lovely Leading Lady, are a diamond, a sparkling gem to the Master Creator, so therefore shine, shine, shine!

CHAPTER 3

The Leading Lady

*"You're supposed to be the Leading Lady
in your own life for God's Sake!"*
KATE WINSLET AS IRIS IN *THE HOLIDAY*.

The Oxford English Dictionary's definition of the *Leading Lady* is **an actress who plays the most important female role in a play or movie.** She is the principal character, the heroine, the prima donna, the diva, or the star of the show. She's the lady the audience takes note of when she graces the screen. If you're anything like me, you like an actor or actress who knows how to fill the screen or the stage with their very presence, and of course, their excellent acting skills! They are so talented, enticing, electrifying, and believable in their ability to embody the character they've chosen or have been selected to play.

They depict their role in such a way that you are

completely enthralled with their performance; they are authentic in their character, and it's quite incredible to see! Some you love and some you love to hate; it depends on their role and the character they portray. Because of her realistic and amazing performances, an actress can become what is known as a "star," nailing the acting completely and embodying the character she endeavored to play compellingly! We applaud her and are grateful for her contribution to the big screen!

She is known to the world as a success both on the screen and in front of the camera. Outside of the glitz and glamor of the flashing lights found in the entertainment industry, her life may be in shambles behind the scenes. However, we celebrate what she can bring to the stage. We are enthralled with her skill to entertain, the ability to make us laugh, cry, or fall in love for the hour and fifty- six minutes we choose to take the time to watch her on-screen. She's motivated by the accolades of people and most assuredly by the payment she receives for her excellent acting skills, which causes her to continue to do what she does and be who she is.

It can be draining, and this in itself can be daunting and even depressing; but she does it anyway, sometimes to the detriment of her personal life and health. So, what makes the leading lady keep driving on in this manner? Why does she continue to do what she does? Because she is a Leading Lady! It's what she's born to do, and it doesn't matter how tired she becomes or how the actual work seems never-ending, she's fulfilled in the doing of it, so she takes pleasure in the journey of it; therefore, she is fueled by the success of it!

Dr. Halene Giddens

*"We need to reshape our own perception
of how we view ourselves. We have to step up
as women and take the lead."*
BEYONCÉ

You are the Leading Lady in your own life, of your own story, and you take the center platform: lights, camera, action! You've got this! I'm writing these words now to let you know that you, my dear sister, are compelling, you're incredible in your own right, and you're amazing! You and I may never perform on the big screen or a grand stage, but we are the "stars" in our own real-time, real-life, action-packed, drama-filled comedy performance. You and I are on center stage in this life we've been afforded the opportunity to live, so we might as well own it. How we "act" in every scene is very important to our achievement and success!

This is not a show for us, or make-believe for us but the real deal, and every moment hereafter counts! We don't just get to take off our makeup, and—ok, well, we do get to take off our makeup; for those of us who wear makeup. Anyway, this is real life, and we should make every effort to live the very best life that we can! This is our life, and we should live it to its full potential; we have been given the opportunity and ability to do just that! Each of us should have the desire deep down on the inside to live a full, overwhelming, excessively blessed life, and it is absolutely ok to want a complete and good life! This is the entirety and whole Will of our Lord: for us to live our lives to the ultimate fullest! This is the goal, and it is absolutely possible to attain it! This is the great gift from our Heavenly Father given through His Son Jesus Christ!

In John 10:10 (AMPC), Jesus said, "I came that they may have and enjoy life, and have it in abundance (to the full, till it overflows)." Our Lord and Savior Jesus Christ gave His Life so that we can have the chance to receive and enjoy a full, abundant life! Both in this natural, earthly experience and in our spiritual connection and journey in our relationship with Him. Spiritual and natural abundance together overflow to us from God along with His Goodness, Glorious Grace, Abundant Favor, Manifold Wisdom, and Overflowing Blessings!

---

*The Lord will give you
an abundance of good things in the land,
just as he promised.*
Deuteronomy 28:11 (TLB)

The abundance of good things is His desired gift for every single one of us, and yes, I mean you as well! I understand that the road thus far may have been hard; it may have even been excruciatingly difficult, which is hard personified. Yet, you're here right now in this present moment of your life, and God's Promise for you is just as real and attainable as for anyone else reading the words on this page!

Our Heavenly Father absolutely did not leave any of us out! I said He did not leave you out of this glorious equation; He's already figured it out for you and has the plan for you! I understand you may already know this, but it's worth reminding you again! He specifically saw you and knew you before you were even in the mind of your mother. He knew and still knows the very real desires and plans He has for you right at this very present moment in time! He is very aware of who you are, and as I just stated, He has the mapped-out plan precisely made just for you!

"I knew you before you were formed within your mother's womb; before you were born I sanctified you and appointed you as my spokesman to the world."
Jeremiah 1:5 (TLB)

For I know the plans I have for you, says the Lord. They are plans for good and not for evil, to give you a future and a hope.
Jeremiah 29:11 (TLB)

Ok, that's a wow! At least it is for me and should be for you! God knew us before we were birthed into this earth realm, and He knows all about us right now in this place and in this space that we are in this very present moment! He's even made specific, special, set aside plans just for you and me! Yes, I'll say it again. That's a big wow: to know that God is concerned about the details of **my** life that He has planned for **me**! So again, you have been given the gift of abundant life; you don't need permission to live this good life. It's already been gifted and granted to you. You are the Leading Lady in this beautiful role called your life, and if you haven't done so up to this point, go ahead and start living it fully!

Every desirable and beneficial gift comes out of heaven.
The gifts are rivers of light cascading down from the
Father of Light. There is nothing deceitful in God,
nothing two-faced, nothing fickle. He brought us to life
using the true Word, showing us off as
the crown of all his creatures.
James 1:17-18 (MSG)

Oh yes, Leading Lady, you are a crown of glory to the Lord, and I can't wait to share more with you about who you are, but first, let's look at a few other Leading Ladies. Now, don't skip ahead; stick with me! If you really want to skip ahead, I can't stop you since you're the one with the book in your hand. Yes, you're the one with the control, so do with it what you will! It's yours!

LEADING LADIES IN THE BIBLE

I find incredible Leading Ladies intertwined in the Word of God. These Leading Ladies fulfilled their God-given assignments here on earth and left a legacy behind them for us to glean from and follow after!

For example, Hannah, though being provoked by her enemy, didn't *clap back*. These enemies or frenemies would be called *haters* in today's vernacular, which is exactly what this other person was to Hannah. If you don't understand the slang, I'll say it this way: Hannah didn't answer the person that continued to provoke her constantly with ugly words.

Though she felt dejected and depressed because she couldn't have children, which was vitally important to her, she went to the temple of the Lord to pray fervently to God with fasting, prayer, and making vows to the Lord.

When Eli, the priest, saw Hannah praying vehemently with her lips moving but no sound coming out of her mouth, he thought she was inebriated because of how she looked in her anguished pleas of desperation! When he confronted Hannah, she explained that she had not been drinking but was crying out to the Lord in prayer. Eli answered her and said, *"May the Lord grant you the petition of your heart."* With that word, Hannah got up from where she was, washed her face from all of the tears, and was no longer depressed and desperate. Instead, she was excited and delighted about the word she heard! She hadn't even received the petition from the Lord that she had so fiercely prayed for, yet she listened to the word and was glad for the word's sake! Meaning, she believed her prayers were answered even before she saw the results manifested, and she was still grateful and thankful!

Months later, she conceived and had a son named Samuel, who became the priest and a prophet of the Lord for all of Israel. He gave counsel to King Saul and King David during his ministry tenure, and this was all due to one woman, a Leading Lady, who became desperate for a promise and didn't give up. Hannah was a Leading Lady persistent in her pursuit to pray until her answer came.

What is the moral of this story? Don't *clap back* at your *haters*; just live your best life and allow God to work things out on your behalf! The true moral of the story is this: the enemy can't stop the purpose and promise God has for you, especially when you're persistent in your faith towards Him! In fact, the true enemy is not the people who may *think* they don't like you because they can do nothing to stop you or the perfect plan God has for your life. The only person that can put a halt to your success, I mean the one person that can cause you to fail and not see great victory in your life, is **YOU**.

Here's what God's Word has to say about you! I know there may be many obstacles placed in front of you; there may have been many disappointments you've experienced in your past. You may be facing a great challenge even right now in your present, but I'm letting you know right now, as if you didn't already know, you can defeat them all! You are the only one stopping you.

"In righteousness you shall be established; you shall be far from oppression, for you shall not fear; and from terror, for it shall not come near you. If anyone stirs up strife, it is not from me; whoever stirs up strife with you shall fall because of you. Behold, I have created the smith who blows the fire of coals and produces a weapon for its purpose. I have also created the ravager to destroy; no weapon that is fashioned against you shall succeed, and you shall refute every tongue that rises against you in judgment. This is the heritage of the servants of the Lord and their vindication from me, declares the Lord."
Isaiah 54:14-17 ESV

God promises that He's got you, especially when you commit and submit to Him. When different things and difficult situations present themselves against you, you have a Heavenly Father who has already formed the weapon against the enemy for your sake! Just for you, so that you can make it through!

Abigail is another example of a beautiful Leading Lady written about in the Old Testament of the Bible. She was married to a fool. Yes, her husband's name was Nabel, which means fool. Due to his pride, arrogance, greed, and contempt for people in general, he almost got his entire family, loved ones, servants, and everyone else under his protection slaughtered. Everyone was close to being annihilated because he wouldn't provide a meal to the soldiers who helped protect his land.

However, due to Abigail's ingenuity, she intercepted the impending peril! She quickly took victuals to the men to appease their leader David, who would soon become the king of Israel and at that very moment, was madder than a hornet! Abigail soothed the savage beast in David and saved her household by speaking words of counsel and wisdom. Boy, that's a wise woman right there! Can you pacify or calm the savage beast in the person that rises up against you with your heartfelt words of wisdom? Do you possess the ability to know what to do and how to operate if the beast in others comes out? We need to take a page from Abigail's story and be the woman of wisdom that knows how to operate when the inevitable happens because, at some point in time, there just may be a beast that you need to confront and comfort. This person could be your boss or your boo; either way, wisdom is the principal thing to help soothe the savage beast.

So anyway, the adventure doesn't end there. That evening, Abigail returns to her home to find Nabel completely smashed, wasted, plastered, and stupefied drunk. He'd thrown himself a huge party that night, so she waited until the next day to explain to him what happened. She shared with her fool of a husband how David, the ultimate warrior, was about to do severe damage to him and everyone concerning him! If she hadn't been alerted to the dismal affair and then, by her ingenuity, intercepted the duplicity, the unthinkable would have happened. Whelp right then and there after hearing the whole story, Nabel had a heart attack, and a few days later, he died. Upon hearing of the fool's death, David traveled back to find Abigail with the beautiful countenance and the right kind of sweet words, married her, and Abigail left all of the foolishness behind.

The moral of this story is just hold on; change is coming, but while you're waiting, make sure you're always a wise woman! When reading the account of Abigail in the Bible, the impression is that what she experienced with Nabel was a common occurrence in one form or another. With discernment and discretion, she had to be a woman of wisdom to maneuver through her marriage to Nabel. For this very reason, the servant who witnessed Nabel going off on David and his men knew immediately to explain to her what happened so that she could handle the matter quickly. Furthermore, the servant knew who to implore on behalf of the entire family. As I stated earlier, wisdom is vital for our lives; it's what we should live by every day in our decision-making process, not *just* in crises, but most especially in the middle of difficult situations. God's Word says a lot about wisdom.

---

*Getting wisdom is the most important thing you can do!
And with your wisdom, develop common sense
and good judgment.*
Proverbs 4:7 (TLB)

What's beautiful about wisdom is we can ask for it.

---

*If you want to know what God wants you to do,
ask him, and he will gladly tell you, for he is always
ready to give a bountiful supply of wisdom to all
who ask him; he will not resent it.*
James 1:5 (TLB)

Our lives will have hardships; the *vicissitudes of life* can be challenging and exciting. Having and operating in wisdom will make the journey easier. Remember, if you lack wisdom, ask for it! Ask God and ask people around you who you know to be wise. Don't lack in Wisdom; ask for Wisdom. You need it, I need it, we all need it, every day.

THE MINISTRY DESPITE THE METHODS

Let's get back to a few other Leading Ladies in the Bible. In some cases with several of these heroines, you may not agree with their methods and motives. You may even wonder what in the world were some of these Leading Ladies thinking!

Say, for instance, the story of Rebekah. She gave birth to two beautiful twin boys. After they became grown men, she plotted with her younger son to steal the birthright of her older son by deceiving their father, Isaac. Ok, yes, she may have figured out that the elder son Esau really had little to no value for spiritual things and that in his heart and mind, he had already sold his birthright to his younger brother Jacob for a bowl of stew! Rebekah may have even had the insight to realize Jacob, although not in the best mental condition at the time emotionally or spiritually, still had a better concept of what God's purpose was for him. We see in the Bible that Jacob was to be the prodigy God would use to bring the 12 tribes, the original people of God, out of his loins. Now that expression "out of his loins" is just a biblical term used to mean God allowed Jacob to produce many sons and daughters. For example, Genesis 46:26 reads, *"All the souls that came with Jacob into Egypt, which came out of his loins, besides Jacob's sons' wives, all the souls were threescore and six."*

As the Leading Lady in her household, Rebekah manipulated and moved the men in her life to bring about the desired results she believed appropriate and right. Now, I wouldn't recommend this as the protocol for the right outcome in the lives of you or your loved ones, as manipulation is never the best or the wisest course of action. Yet, as we see when we continue to read the account, Esau went from hating and wanting to kill Jacob for his deceitfulness to loving his little brother again because God increased them both in their later years.

Although it wasn't the best-laid plan for a mother to deceive her husband and sons, God used it anyway. Even when we don't get it right and we most definitely, completely get it wrong, God can fix it, fix us and make it work for us. Maybe Rebekah's thought was, *"I was trying to do the right thing even though I went about it in the wrong way."* I wonder if she got any points for that. I hope so, because I don't know about you, but I can mess up some things at times, too! Perhaps not to this degree, but in some areas of our lives, we can make mistakes and, praise God, we can believe God to clean up and make up for our mess ups. It may take some time, like with this family, but God *can* make it up for us!

THE BLESSING INSTEAD OF THE TURMOIL

Here's another Leading Lady whose tactics used may not have been what some would call copacetic. Let's share a little bit of her story. Our matriarch is Sarai, which means princess. God changed her name to Sarah, which means noblewoman. The simple name change is indicative of the value God places on our growth, maturity, and development: A princess being at one level of honor and prestige, then, over time, advancing to the next level of nobility, which is an elevation in hierarchy, grandeur, and excellence.

(I'd just like to place a parenthetical pause right here, hence why this paragraph is placed in parentheses. This is exactly how your Heavenly Father sees you! You are His princess! He desires you to develop into the noble, intelligent, grand woman of excellence that He has destined and designed you to be! In the New Testament, the Bible calls us daughters of Sara (1 Peter 3:6). If we are daughters, then what's given to the mother as an inheritance belongs to each of us. Therefore, you are a noblewoman of high honor and value; this is precisely how God our Creator sees you.)

I just had to interrupt this narration to share this truth with you! And here's the scripture verse to amplify this fact!

An excellent woman [one who is spiritual, capable, intelligent, and virtuous], who is he who can find her? Her value is more precious than jewels, and her worth is far above rubies or pearls.
Proverbs 31:10 AMP

I'll repeat it—in case you read it too fast. You are valuable, you are of high quality, and you are priceless! Oh, yes, you are, you lovely and beautiful lady!

Let's continue to observe Sarah. She told Abraham, her husband, to sleep with her servant girl Hagar! Saying, *"Maybe that's what God meant when He said He was giving us a child."* As we discover when reading further along in the Bible, that's not what God meant. By the way, He doesn't need any help fulfilling the promises He has for you either. He only requires your faith, hope, trust, and belief in Him. Here's an excerpt from that folly!

So Sarai said to Abram, "The LORD has prevented me from having children. Go and sleep with my servant. Perhaps I can have children through her." And Abram agreed with Sarai's proposal. So Sarai, Abram's

> *wife, took Hagar the Egyptian servant and gave her*
> *to Abram as a wife. (This happened ten years after*
> *Abram had settled in the land of Canaan.)*
> Genesis 16:2-3 (NLT)

I know, right! Absolute craziness! But we can't judge Sarah too harshly. Actually, we shouldn't judge her at all. This type of behavior or practice was customary for this time period, so she wasn't completely out of line or totally out of her mind. She just came up with her own plan, which she thought was quite reasonable and apparently doable. And she also thought she would get the desired result they both so desperately wanted in the time frame they wanted it in, which was in their estimation as close to "right now" as they could possibly get. I did mention something about having our own plan at the beginning of this book. So, you can go back right now and take a look at that if you just happened to miss it on your way to this third chapter.

Ok, let's go on. If you read the narration in its entirety, you will see that although Abraham and Sarah missed the Lord in this regard, God still fulfilled His promise to them and through them. That gives you and me hope that although we don't always get things precisely right the first, second, and sometimes third time, God still has a promise for us to fulfill. And that's Good News! We just need to get ourselves in line and aligned with the plan. What plan, you may be wondering? God's plan for our lives, our family, and our future.

Apostle Holcomb used to say to us quite frequently, *"Stop trying to figure out what only God can work out!"* In other words, let

God work this thing out for you! The older generation would put it this way, *"You're going to hurt yourself trying to mess with things that are too high for you to figure out or even understand."* I do not have that quoted correctly, but you know what I mean. Let me allow King David to speak on the matter.

LORD, my heart is not proud;
my eyes are not haughty. I don't concern myself with
matters too great or too awesome for me to grasp.
Instead, I have calmed and quieted myself,
like a weaned child who no longer cries for
its mother's milk. Yes, like a weaned child
is my soul within me.
Psalms 131:1-2 (NLT)

David is saying here, *"Lord, I am in complete contentment in allowing You to work things out for me."* He says, *"just like a child who has developed enough to be weaned from their mother's breast and no longer cries for what the child can no longer have, I'm going to be quiet and at peace with whatever happens next for me."* We can't always understand everything, but we can allow God to work out all things.

Oh, and by the way, since we're comparing Leading Ladies on the screen to the Leading Lady in you, every actor or actress working in a series usually has no idea how their character's exact plot will turn out. Nevertheless, a great actress still gives the performance their all; she pours herself into the role! So you, my dear Leading Lady, must also give your all in the performance of your life, not always knowing all the particulars or the plot twists and turns that take place from one season to the next. That's the real beauty of your life's plan being in His Hand because He will work it all out in you, for you, and even through you if you let Him! Just give it your all, give it your best, and be assured that your God will indeed work out the rest!

And we know [with great confidence] that God [who is deeply concerned about us] causes all things to work together [as a plan] for good for those who love God, to those who are called according to His plan and purpose.
Romans 8:28 AMP

I'll also put this right here: every single one of us is called according to God's plan and purpose; every single one of us, and He hasn't left any of us out of His plan. I'll say it again: not one of you lovely ladies is left out of God's plan!

VICTORY AT THE HANDS OF LEADING LADIES

Here's another biblical Leading Lady, Deborah, who was a Prophetess in the days of the Judges. During this time in biblical history, the nation of Israel had no king, so the Judges in that day ruled the country. According to the report concerning Deborah, she was married to a man named Lapidoth; the scriptures do not describe her husband as a leader of any significance. He was not a prophet, priest, king, or nobleman. Instead, he was the man behind the woman, the man standing with the woman of God. He was the man who was married to the prophetess, who was the first and only female judge who sat and dwelt in the space of property that was named after her; yep, it was called Deborah, plain and simple.

According to the scriptures, because of the blatant acts of evil the people of God consistently committed, the Israelite people experienced severe oppression from their enemies for over 20 years in this particular period. During this time, Deborah sat down right where she was and judged all of Israel. This meant men and women from throughout the entire populace came from near and far to receive counsel, wisdom, and instruction from her continually. I especially love what Deborah says concerning herself after she leads an army to fight against the hard affliction of their enemy and wins! Yes, you read it right; she led an army that was outnumbered and outmatched into battle against their enemy! She called on a man named Barak and said, *"Hasn't God commanded you to lead the armies against the oppressor, and God will cause you to defeat the enemy who has come against us!"*

Although the prophetic word came from Deborah to give to Barak, he said, *"The only way I'm going into this battle is if you go with me."* Without hesitation, Deborah's response assured Barak. *"I'll surely go with you, but the entire victorious outcome will come from the hand of a woman."* That woman's name was Jael. She took a tent nail and thrust it through the head of the general leading the army coming against the children of Israel...while he slept, in fact! Exhausted from the battle against Barak and his men, the general went into her tent because he knew her husband and there was supposed to be some kind of peace treaty between them. But this little lady said, *"I see an awesome opportunity here, and I'm going to take it!"*

78

So, she invited that general into her tent and said, *"I gotcha now,"* and voila! Victory for an entire nation was completed and done!

After the battle was won, Prophetess Deborah sang a song! God had given them success through the hands of two willing women who took the lead!

> *"In the days of Shamgar, son of Anath,*
> *In the days of Jael, The highways were deserted,*
> *And the travelers walked along the byways.*
> *Village life ceased, it ceased in Israel,*
> *Until I, Deborah, arose, Arose a mother in Israel."*
> Judges 5:6-7 (NKJV)

Deborah said that she arose, she arose as a mother in Israel! She saw the horrible treatment of her people, and she said, *"I've got to get up and do something!"* She was already the judge and the prophet, but she got up from that calling and became the mother of a nation!

Let me tell you something; there's more in you than you think! I will say it again: there is so much more in you than you can even imagine! I know you thought you were one thing, and even some believe they're nothing, but I'm letting you know right now, my precious sweet sister, there is so much more in you than you first believed! There is so much more in you than you can even conceive! There is so much more in you than you have expected to receive; this means there are still things that need to come up out of you! Some of you haven't even begun to tap into the profundity and depth of all you are and all you're supposed to do and be! I genuinely hope you're internalizing these words right now.

Like I said earlier, don't try to figure it out right now. Just let God work it out when the time is right. Deborah had to get up from where she was sitting, and my friend, you've got to get up, too! Get up from your mentality of the mundane! Get up from complacency! Get up from complaining about things around you that need to change. Instead, be the change! You may say, what can I do, what do I have that can make any kind of real change? Well, Jael used a tent nail!

The scriptures talk about a man named Shamgar. He was a farmer who later became a judge over Israel because he found what he could do right where he was! He killed 600 Philistines with an ox goad, which is a farming utensil. He turned something used to poke and prod oxen in the fields into a weapon against the enemy. He used what he had in his hand just as Jael used what she had in her hand!

It's not just about what's in your wallet; it's also about what's in your hand, what's in your heart, and what's in your head! Look at these things, examine the value of your amazing talents and giftings and use what God has given you to bring about the change you want to be and the change you'd like to see! It's already in you to be what you've always been destined to be! This thing in you, Leading Lady, just needs to be cultivated, and it may need to be calibrated, balanced out, and aligned with God's true design. Then you may just be compensated in some form or fashion just because you used what you already have, you started right in the place you already are, and you're doing what you're able to do already! It's in you! I promise you. It just needs to come up out of you!

By the way, I think making up victory songs after a major battle is an amazing idea, and we should all try it. We may even need to make a victory song *before* the trial or the struggle. This will help us get through the tough times we encounter! We sing songs that make us happy to get through difficult situations we face, and we absolutely should! Sing when you're happy, sing when you're not so happy; sing in the good times and do what you can to lift up a song even when times are hard. We should especially lift up a song when we've come on the other side of a major event or great milestone in our lives. That's exactly what Mariam, Moses and Aaron's sister, did when the Israelite people crossed over the Red Sea on dry ground, as recounted in the book of Exodus.

The horses of Pharaoh, his horsemen, and his chariots tried to follow through the sea; but the Lord let down the walls of water on them while the people of Israel walked through on dry land. Then Miriam the prophetess, the sister of Aaron, took a tambourine and led the women in dances. And Miriam sang this song: Sing to the Lord, for he has triumphed gloriously. The horse and rider have been drowned in the sea.
Exodus 15:19-21 (TLB)

The point of this depiction I'm sharing right now is, first of all, we didn't even know Mariam was a prophetess until she picked up her tambourine and started leading a praise dance with singing! I mean, really, who knew? Until that very moment, Moses and the people of God were glorifying God in singing and dancing. The next thing we read, Mariam leads the women in a prophetic praise dance while singing praises to God. You just might be surprised! Who knows what will come out of you when you allow yourself the opportunity to be used in the plan of God.

My second point to this is: sing your way through your trial, sing your way out of it as well and then sing right up to the moment you see your victory on the horizon. It doesn't matter if you know how to sing, just get some good music together and sing! I had to share this; if you're feeling low, sing. If you're feeling just ok, sing, and if you're feeling well, go ahead, lift up a good inspiring song, and sing, sing, sing!

Dr. Halene Giddens

CHAPTER 4

Leading Ladies By Example And Most Importantly The Leading Lady In You!

"Leadership is not a person or a position.
It is a complex moral relationship
between people based on trust, obligation,
commitment, emotion, and a shared vision of the good."
JOANNE CIULLA

Let's look at a couple of Leading Ladies with us presently, along with those from our past.

Former First Lady Michelle LaVaughn Obama was, of course, the first African American or woman of color to grace the highest seat in our nation as the wife of the 44th President of the United States, Barack Obama. Regardless of your political affiliation or association, if you've heard or read even a little bit about her, you can attest to the fact that she's one woman that can be looked up to with respect and pride. It doesn't matter your nationality or background; I believe she has something to offer anyone who may follow her career.

Michelle Obama is an American attorney and author who graduated from Princeton University and Harvard Law School. She hails from the Southside of Chicago, a region predominantly made up of people of color. Most African Americans from Chicago are from the southside. It was the more impoverished region, the urban district; everything about it was opposite the Caucasian neighborhood on the other side of the proverbial tracks, if you would. According to my mother, who is also from Chicago by way of Mobile, Alabama, there wasn't anything particularly negative about growing up there; it's just the way things were as described by those from there. I find that Mrs. Obama embodied the highest degree of proficiency and grace in the midst of severe and constant strain of criticism on a national level amassed upon herself and her husband.

I absolutely love her glow and her flow; she's striking and carries a charismatic strength. In an age where it may be challenging to find women of color to emulate and look up to, Michelle Obama can visibly be seen as a leading lady with class and style. This is not to say there are no other women in our communities, families, churches, and workplaces we look up to as beautiful examples of ladies who lead in their realm. But, on the national and international level, I'm simply pointing out that we may be able to identify with her as a leading lady who's paving the way for all of us to follow.

Michelle Obama is an example of a woman who uses courage and strength to succeed. As we have seen, the limelight and constant scrutiny of an entire nation and the whole world at large has to be an undertaking of immeasurable stress, anxiety, and pressure on any person in any position. Yet, she was able to endure all of it, she and the former President together. Some of their writings have mentioned the toll political life has taken on their marital relationship. However, even through the pressure, the persona remains of what looks to be a beautiful and healthy marriage.

Knowing that any misstep or a wrong move could cause their political world to be obliterated right before their eyes, they had to live above reproach in every aspect of their lives, even right now. For the Obamas to have any voice or write a single word on a page of a book presumes they have been examined by the press, their colleagues, and perhaps family and friends finding them without blame. In this day and age, that's quite remarkable. Their marriage, money, families, and their lineage have been looked upon and judged in every form and fashion, yet they have been able to come across, if you would, squeaky clean.

Now, we know that there are no perfect people and there

is no perfect marital union. We understand marriage is a continued ongoing work in the process of learning and loving each other and letting the small things that really shouldn't matter go. Marriage is also about preferring the other above ourselves—a practice that, of course, should be reciprocated. This simply means doing what we can to make the other reasonably happy to the best of our ability. It's the capacity to grow and mature with our spouse, to build a relationship with the one we say we want to spend the rest of our lives with. It's the resigned determination to realize our spouse is the one with whom we are supposed to build our lives, recognizing that we are better together. Besides all of this, can you imagine? Everything becomes magnified when the spotlight is on you all the time, as with the former first couple.

The Obamas have almost kind of made it look easy, the marriage, the political life, all of it. As I stated, regardless of whether or not you supported every decision that came through the White House or you were furious at the legislation that passed during their tenure in office, you've got to respect the couple for endurance's sake. They made it look pretty charming like the days of Camelot with Jackie O and former President John F. Kennedy. The Obamas have been compared to them because they were both a bit young as the President and First Lady of what's known as the "free world." This beautiful couple was and still is both charming and a President and First Lady who truly wanted to be for the people, all of the people; this was always their perspective and goal. The Kennedys embodied this same sentiment as well to an extent.

But as we've come to discover through the years, the Kennedys' life was no fairy tale. Yet, I still admire Jacqueline

Kennedy Onassis. I won't mention all she may have endured while married to President John Fitzgerald Kennedy. Being the wife behind the man, beside the man, and even sometimes in front of the man is never an easy endeavor. Of course, this can also depend on the kind of man you're married to—so I won't go on about their marriage, especially since I wasn't there, and I don't know the whole story. I wanted to mention Jackie O because she held herself with such dignity and grace through it all. I do know she's not the only lady who had to bear up against such obstacles in their marital relationship. But with all of the scrutiny, several miscarriages, and other hardships, she seemed to show strength of character through it.

As I've stated, marriage isn't always easy, but if two people can make the decision to please God by pleasing each other, then marriage can be positively beautiful. It's really what God desires for us, to be pleased and pleasing with our lifelong partner.

DESTINY FLOURISHES WITHIN OUR DISABILITY

I can't stop! I'm on a roll! Here are two other leading ladies I've always secretly admired in my heart and mind! Helen Keller, wow! What about her teacher Anne Sullivan? Now, she had a no-quit, fighting spirit if I've ever heard of one as Ms. Keller's teacher and lifelong friend! A positively extraordinary legacy, and if you haven't read her story, perhaps you've seen the movie about Helen Keller's life!

It was positively riveting to see her struggle and perseverance through it! Helen Adams Keller became blind and deaf due to illness as a very young child. Not hearing or seeing inhibited her from speaking and communicating, which, of course, frustrated her to no end! What's amazing is she was the first deaf-blind person to graduate from college in 1904, and she graduated cum laude, which means she graduated third, yes third, of her class! She became an author, disability rights advocate, political activist, and lecturer, traveling all over the country and the world.

Another reason her life completely inspires me is because of the woman who didn't give up on her, Anne Sullivan, her first teacher, who taught her language, reading, and writing. I'm enthralled by the patience and persistence to absolutely never give up on Ms. Keller regardless of how difficult it was to reach and teach her. Did Ms. Sullivan see the potential in Ms. Keller, or did she just want to give her a chance to communicate with her family and others around her? Anne Sullivan had to be driven in her determination to provide Helen Keller with the opportunity she needed to learn so that she'd have a voice to speak to the world. Did Anne realize what would be released from Helen when she taught her how to receive an education?

Nothing's more important to us as human beings than to be able to communicate with one another, to share in fellowship with one another, to have a voice, and to be heard. To listen to people and to be able to respond intelligently. To understand and to be understood. It's how we bond with others around us; it's how we formulate and forge friendships and function in our families. And as you know, we like to be able to talk and get our point across, to give and exchange thoughts. Anne Sullivan gave Helen Keller the vital and much-desired tools she needed to place her on the road to fulfill her God-given destiny! And what a lifelong legacy for these two leading ladies to leave behind!

> *"The best and most beautiful things*
> *in this world cannot be seen or even heard,*
> *but must be felt with the heart."*
> HELEN KELLER

MADAM VICE PRESIDENT

Attorney General of California, United States Senator, Madam Vice President Kamala Devi Harris made history. Again, putting aside our political thoughts and views, this is "breaking through the glass ceiling" big. The first female to sit in the second highest seat in our nation and the first person of color to hold the office of Vice President. Kamala Harris overcame barriers to become the first woman, first Black, and first Asian-American Vice President in the United States.

Ms. Harris is from Oakland, California, where she was raised in a single-family home by her Indian mother, Shyamala Gopalan Harris. She graduated from Howard University, a Historically Black College and University (HBCU) that predominantly focuses on African American students' academic learning and higher education. Again, you may not agree with her politics or policies, and you can believe what you want about her road to the White House, but this is a breakthrough for all women, women of color, young girls, teen girls, and ladies of all ages. The motto is if she can do it, we can do it, too, and the next time just may be bigger and better!

YOU ARE THE LEADING LADY

"If you need to see something gorgeous and amazing today,
for no particular reason, look in a mirror."
ELIZABETH GILBERT

A Leading Lady is any woman who leads in any capacity, whether she is a business manager or a micromanager. This means she manages her own life on some level or another, which, of course, is every single woman on the planet. Whether she has a title and position in commerce or is not even recognized in that realm of service, a Leading Lady is inside her. You, yes, you, are a Leading Lady in the home and outside of it; you're leading in some facet or another.

In this book, I hope you are being inspired and encouraged to take the lead, discovering who you are and what you have on the inside of you. Really that's what we ladies must do, should do, and have the privilege of doing, to lead and live our lives to the fullest. Whatever aspect we live in, we've got to take the lead. Most importantly, over our own life, body, mind, and soul! You are a Leading Lady. It's not important what you may believe, the greatness or the smallness of your area of achievement, or what your status may or may not be, a Leading Lady you most especially are!

"Believe in yourself even when you're being challenged
by your thoughts, people, and tough situations.
Be strong. You got this!"
SUCCESS MINDED

Leading or leadership looks different and works differently

in and for everyone. We all have distinct and separate personalities that make leadership very diverse. So, let's recognize that unique quality in ourselves and realize we are, in fact—yes, you lovely lady—are classified in what I'd like to refer to as a Leading Lady!

When I look at myself as a Leading Lady, I lead alongside my husband in ministry. Therefore, my decision-making and leadership approach complement and does not contradict his leadership style and delivery. Sometimes this can be tricky, even at best. Some of the time, it takes tact, and all the time, it takes me treasuring the gift my husband is to me and the gift I am to him, which can be complex because sometimes I forget. Sometimes I want to do my own thing my way. I get impatient, and I want things now. At that precise moment, I get anxious and restless. That's when I take a deep breath, get myself together, and talk to myself about tact, time, and when both need to be employed.

By the way, all great leaders talk to themselves. I know you talk to yourself at least some of the time. How do you think a leader fleshes out their plans and problems? They talk to themselves and talk to other great leaders about what great leaders need to be: great leaders! So, here's another little nugget: find a good leader to follow, so you can find out what leading in your arena looks like and what it takes to be a good and later a great leader.

And while you're allowing them to help you, take from them correction, direction, and instruction; you can't get better unless you're challenged to do so. This is good food for thought, so you should probably go ahead and eat it. Anyway, as I was saying, leadership looks different and is managed differently with each person. There is no cookie-cutter cut out to employ a particular leadership style; it's all about being the best you that God created you to be! And this I know for sure, God has most definitely created you to be a leading lady who's a good leader in your own right.

Although your guiding light, the mentor and motivator you may choose to follow after, is someone you'd like to in a sense emulate, yet and still, you're not going to be exactly like that person. Your personality is different, your qualities are not exactly the same, and that's ok; it really is! We shouldn't be copies and clones because we've been created with special attributes that are our own. Embrace those attributes, care for and cultivate those things that make you uniquely you; they're beautiful, they're lovely, they're you! We're not perfect, and that's ok, too. We should always strive to get and be better, so even at my failed attempts, mishaps, and mistakes, I'm still a leading lady, and so are you!

> *"The quality of a Leader is reflected*
> *in the standards they set for themselves."*
> **RAY KROC**

To *lead* simply means *to move forward by taking a person or persons by the hand or to show someone the way to a destination by going in front of them or walking beside them*. It also means *to influence or to induce for a cause or a certain position taken, to guide in course, direction, action, or opinion*. A leader is an influencer, and every lady has had the opportunity and/or privilege to influence someone whether they recognize this or not. And haven't we all had the opportunity to be and do just that over the course of our lives, for the positive or the negative? Ok, let's be honest for a sec; every course of action we take is not necessarily for our betterment. We occasionally may make a mistake or two or three or four; shall I go on? No? Great!

All I'm saying is, Ladies, you are leaders, and you are leading. It's in you to lead. We just need to know who we are and what we have working inside us so that we may lead effectively! I believe it may be why we as women bump heads so often with each other, which ought not to be so. Yet, unfortunately, this happens at times. If we had a real understanding of who we are, what we have, and what we're working with, we would be able to work with each other. We could encircle each other as women when needed by functioning and cohabitating in collaboration with the idea of being and doing better with and for each other! That was a mouthful, I know. But I needed to get it all in.

As I go on, I'm not saying we as women can't and don't work together for the most part. I'm pointing out that after engaging with women in different age brackets, ethnicities, and varying levels of Christianity to non-Christians, issues do ensue from time to time. I'm just saying. So, it is an area where we can use some empowerment to be more aware of it, face it, deal with it, and most especially conquer this issue.

Ladies, it's because we are leaders, and sometimes we don't take kindly to being told what to do, when to do it, how to do it, where to do it, you know all of that. But, there's a gifting in us that can and should be used for the good because it is absolutely in each one of us! Just like any grace gift and talent, it can be and should be developed, nourished, nurtured, and made better by following good examples of ladies and even gentlemen you know to be leaders in your realm of influence.

And sometimes—yep, sometimes—seeing what not to do by paying attention to others who have gone before you and have not made the wisest decisions when it comes to their own lives and perhaps leadership style, this will help you along the way. Observation of those around you in front and behind you is excellent data collection for future reference for your personal leadership training. It's all learning and development. It's all helpful for you and me to be and do better. Leadership is a learned skill if practiced and taken to heart. We can bring improvement to any area of our lives. Every one of us has it in us to be and do better. It's a God-given mechanism in us to strive to be more and do more! It's in you!

AND HERE'S ANOTHER THOUGHT

Before we go on to the next chapter, I'd like to share this thought with you. Our growth and development take time. The key is to get started!

> *"It doesn't matter when you start,*
> *it doesn't matter where you start.*
> *All that matters is that you start."*
> SIMON SINEK

IT TAKES TIME

I received this thought from a chapter I read in Gloria Copeland's *Hidden Treasures*, a devotional written in 1998 on the

94

book of Proverbs. She is a Christian minister and bestselling author known worldwide for teaching millions of people the principles of faith and healing found in the Bible. Along with her husband, Kenneth Copeland, she founded Kenneth Copeland Ministries in Fort Worth, Texas, and they have been in ministry together for over 50 years.

Hidden Treasures is a 31-day devotional exploring the wisdom keys found in the book of Proverbs in the Bible. She used the following scripture:

Dishonest money dwindles away,
but whoever gathers money little by little makes it grow.
Proverbs 13:11 NIV

The Law of Gradual Increase is this: when you obtain the things that you desire little by little, inch by inch, step by step, the more you can make room to grow and increase and truly, the more you understand and appreciate what you've received! It does make a difference. Another translation of this verse of scripture says, *"wealth gotten in haste or too quickly will soon dwindle away, but he who gathers little by little will increase his riches."* This is a wisdom key for the soul. Here's another excellent explanation in a different translation.

Easy come, easy go,
but steady diligence pays off.
Proverbs 13:11 (MSG)

We live in a world that wants and receives everything fast. Sometimes we don't want to put in the time to achieve or receive success in certain areas of our lives. Or we put some time in, and if we don't see immediate results or change, we drop it and start something else. We want it quick, and we want it fast; we want it now! We don't just want what we want today! We want it yesterday or the day before, or the day before that! I want to spin around, look in the mirror, like the Disney princesses, and instantly be changed, instantly be transformed, instantly be new! That's what I want! Instantly, I look and feel better. Instantly, I've got the dream job. Instantly, I have a great marriage. I tithed once, and, instantly, my money is better. Have you noticed that all those princesses had to go through something to get to their instant change in those cute Disney movies? It's just how the story goes!

You know there are so many weight loss workouts, eating plans, diets, and healthy choices we can embark upon, and my husband likes to tell me that every single one of them works, I guarantee you that! You just gotta keep working it! I don't know about you, but I've tried a few, and I can attest to the fact they've all worked for me. Yep, every one of them at some point or another worked, some slowly, very slowly, and some a little quicker. But, unfortunately, I just didn't keep working. I got tired, burnt out, lazy.

No matter how much you want,
laziness won't help a bit, but hard work
will reward you with more than enough.
Proverbs 13:4 CEV

What?! So, if I'm lazy, I won't get what I want, but if I work hard, I'll get a reward! Well, that seems easy enough! But that's just it: it's not easy. It's hard and takes hard work! It takes time! It takes consistency! It takes diligence! I gotta work it to get it!

---

*Lazy people want much but get little,
while the diligent are prospering.*
Proverbs 13:4 TLB

Oh, my goodness! Wow! That's a home run hitter with this translation here! Now, that is not just in our financial situation. This word can be applied to every aspect of our lives, spiritually and naturally! In our growth with God, in relationships, on the job, in church and at home, even with our spouse if we're married, or with anyone, we can apply this when it comes to our thought processes as well as with our physical bodies! If it's going to work, we've got to work it! My desire and hope for you is that you find your art of practicing greatness—the motivation that causes you to keep it pushing.

Working towards our fabulous future, desired goals, and projected perfected plans is never an easy process. It is sometimes steady-as-you-go. Yet, as we embark on our future success journey, we can be assured if we remain diligent, even if it's up-down and sometimes all around, we'll make it to the other side (Matthew 14:22)! Keep moving; don't stop unless it's to take a breather and rest awhile. Fulfilling your destiny is a *systematic series of actions, a continuous operation going toward a definitive course*, again called the process. It's the method it takes to achieve results! As I stated—and I repeat myself quite a bit—leading is in you; it really is. So, take the lead because you are a Leading Lady!

"Never be afraid to try something new! Remember, amateurs built the Ark. Professionals built the Titanic."
AUTHOR UNKNOWN

Let me infuse this statement into your hearts and minds as I'm thinking about it right now! This is for all the saved, sanctified, set-aside sistah's, which is every single one of you who says "Yes" to Jesus! You are immediately saturated, made secure, and assured of success by His saving grace being formed as a whole in you, completely lacking nothing! And that's good news! I hope you receive the magnitude of this statement. It's what gives you your superb status to achieve the greatness that's in you simply because of God's graciousness and holiness covering you! He is your Promise Keeper, and if you let Him, He will keep you from falling, so you can take this lead (Jude 1:24).

Dr. Halene Giddens

CHAPTER 5

Attributes Of The Leading Lady

"If your actions create a legacy
that inspires others to dream more,
learn more, do more and become more,
then, you are an excellent leader."
DOLLY PARTON

In the previous chapter, we discussed Leading Ladies in larger-than-life roles. You know the ladies we can see but not touch? They make a great impact but from a great distance. I'd like to mention a few ladies, and only just a few because there are so many in my life that I can actually reach out and touch and have touched me in an impactful way.

When I talk about Leading Ladies, I have to mention my mom, Pearline Nealy Chamberlayne. She is positively hilarious with all of the life stories she's shared with me throughout my childhood into adulthood. At the time of writing this book, my mom is 88 years old, and she's seen and experienced so much in her lifetime. Each time we talk, she shares a little more of her story with me. Some things are extremely sad and difficult, while some things are extremely happy and exciting. Still, some things are extremely funny, and of course, that's my favorite part. All in all, mom says she's had a great life, especially the life she was able to share with my dad, which she always likes to express to me. Mom always likes to let me know my dad wasn't perfect, and of course, neither was she, but they loved each other for 54 years before he passed away, and she misses him dearly.

When I told my mom I was finally writing a book, she said, "Oh, you should write about me and maybe your grandmother." Now, there's a grand dame if ever I've met one! My grandmother Helen Louise (Bassett) Hornsby was a bit of a matchmaker in her latter years, and those would be a few funny stories to tell. I think if I wrote about these two ladies, it would definitely be a comedy with a few sad parts, with the sad parts being a part of the whole story, but aren't all great comedies filled with both? Maybe one day I'll share their story; I don't know, we'll see. My grandmother said, "Everyone has at least one good book in them," she wrote a couple of books herself. I know we all have stories of people who have touched and affected our lives in tremendous ways. We need to commit these lovely ones to our memories and keep them close to our hearts.

My mother-in-law or my mother-in-love, Tawanna Giddens Peoples—mother-in-love is what I like to call her when I mention her to others; she is strength personified; that's what I see in her. You have to be strong to raise two strong children on your own. Even though she had help from her mother, the bulk of the rearing and upbringing came from her. It really does take a community of people to raise children, or at least it should. When I look at mothers with small children, I'm always in awe. First of all, I think, "My goodness, that was once me," and then I think, "Little people have an abundance of energy which is completely amazing!" I go on to think, "The stamina and ingenuity it takes to rear and raise these little people are incredible!" Finally, I close this inner discourse with, "I'm sure glad that isn't me anymore!"

Right now, I'm praying for multiplied grace and strength to all of the mothers, grandmothers, stepmothers, and those who are standing in as mothers! May you know beyond a shadow of a doubt that your labor is not in vain! You are making an impact on the lives and in the lives of your little ones in everything you do. Even as they become older, your words and your work matter. It may not always be visible in them or their actions, but be assured your Heavenly Father sees your labor of love, and you will be rewarded for your faithfulness!

I salute all the single mothers doing their very best to raise their children. You are to be commended and celebrated, loved and cherished, and I hope you know you are absolutely all of these things! If no one has told you lately or at all, you are loved, cherished, celebrated, and you are noticed. Your Heavenly Father sees you, He knows you, He hears you, and He most especially loves you! So, take a moment to breathe that in; take a moment to allow His Strength to be imparted in you to strengthen and empower you to keep pressing forward.

KEEP PRESSING FORWARD! Whether single or married, with or without kids, ladies keep going and keep growing because victory isn't around the corner; victory is yours right now! You have the victory because the Victorious One lives in you. So don't stop! Keep moving! Get your rest when you can, and then get back up! You are more than conquerors; you are victorious!

VICTORIOUS EVEN THROUGH MISTAKES

Yet even in the midst of all these things,
we triumph over them all, for God has made us to be
more than conquerors, and his demonstrated love is our
glorious victory over everything!
Romans 8:37 TPT

Come on, Woman of God, receive that resilient strength to press on and go on! It's already in you to conquer and be victorious! God has placed it in you; you have everything you need to be failproof! This, of course, doesn't mean we won't mess up or make mistakes! Every one of us misses it throughout our life's journey, sometimes once or twice a day! It's ok!

"Mistakes are part of the dues
one pays for a full life."
SOPHIA LOREN

*"Learning by making mistakes and
not duplicating them is what life is about."*
LINDSAY FOX

Here's one of the best quotes about mistakes, in my opinion!

*"Learn from the mistakes of others.
You can't live long enough to make them all yourself."*
ELEANOR ROOSEVELT

Although we walk around with our mistake-making selves, we are still God's favored girls.

PASTOR VALERIE IVY HOLCOMB

Ok, just one more lovely lady who's been an amazing Leading Lady I've looked up to is my mother in the faith, Pastor Valerie Ivy Holcomb, the wife of the late Apostle Nate Holcomb. Together they pastored the Christian House of Prayer (CHOP) in the central Texas area for over 38 years before Apostle Holcomb went home to be with the Lord. My husband and I, along with our children, were members of CHOP before moving to California and starting Destiny Christian Center. We have stayed connected to this man and woman of God for 30 plus years! We are so grateful to God that He saw fit to place us in their ministry, and our lives have been forever changed because of our covenant connection!

Since Apostle Holcomb's transition to Heaven, Pastor Valerie leads at the helm of a ministry God committed to their care with over 3,000 members. She also oversees an organization of 400 ministers and ministries all over the United States and abroad. I've been able to see her occasionally up close and personal. She's humble, human, spiritual, real, and a beautiful woman of God. She has a dual grace on her life as a businesswoman running the inner working of ministry and as a spiritual leader giving continued guidance and encouragement to all who call upon her.

As a mentor, both up close and even from afar, I'm so honored and humbled to have her in my life. She is an astounding example of strength, intelligence, and courage under fire. No matter what she faces or what faces her, she keeps going, pressing, and moving forward. She is a lady who most assuredly knows how to lead.

QUALITIES AND CHARACTERISTICS OF THE LEADING LADY

"Leadership is a series of behaviors rather than a role for heroes."
MARGARET WHEATLEY

Let's look at some qualities and characteristics of the Leading Lady. These attributes are developed over time with God's help because He always wants to lead, assist and guide us. These characteristics have already been placed in us by the help of the Holy Spirit. They can be released through us because they are already right here inside of us, waiting to be ignited in us. Development is essential to the success of your God-given, God-inspired exceptional capabilities! First, let me give you the six characteristics. Now, please don't cringe or get turned off by any of these; I promise we'll get through them all together in the next few chapters. Here are the six:

The Leading Lady Sees
The Leading Lady Speaks
The Leading Lady Stands
The Leading Lady Surrenders
The Leading Lady Sacrifices
The Leading Lady Submits

THE LEADING LADY SEES

If people can't see what God is doing,
they stumble all over themselves;
But when they attend to what he reveals,
they are most blessed.
Proverbs 29:18 (MSG)

Seeing is very important to perception. This word *perception* is *the state of being or process of becoming aware of something through the senses*. This definition depicts the external sensory realm. *Perception* is also defined as an *intuitive recognition of moral, psychological, or aesthetic qualities pertaining to intuition, insight, and discernment*. This definition deals with awareness, consciousness, and impressions, something a little deeper than seeing with our natural eyes. Sight in both realms is a God-given gift to us, although there's another level of seeing our Heavenly Father desires for us to operate from.

In our everyday lives, we would say seeing is necessary for

functionality. Still, when we look at the life of Helen Keller, we understand that seeing naturally or seeing with our physical eyes is not necessarily needed to thrive. So, what type of seeing is vital for us? First of all, let's qualify: you are not just flesh and bone. There is so much more to you than what we see with natural eyes. You are a spiritual being.

Every one of us, whether we are saved, which is the born-again experience received by knowing Jesus Christ as your Lord and Savior, or whether we haven't fully acknowledged or committed our lives to Jesus Christ, we are all three-part beings. Spirit, soul, and body. We are, first of all, spirit beings, we've been given a soul, and we live in a physical body. Our physical bodies are just the earth suit we've been given to live in on this earth. Since this planet is not our permanent place of residence, we might as well acknowledge we have other aspects of ourselves that we're working with.

---

*Now, may the God of peace and harmony set you apart,
making you completely holy. And may your entire
being —spirit, soul, and body —be kept completely
flawless in the appearing of our Lord Jesus,
the Anointed One. The one who calls you by name
is trustworthy and will thoroughly
complete his work in you.*
1 Thessalonians 5:23-24 (TPT)

In proving the point, I had to add verse 24 because Jesus Christ has called you by name, and He wants to complete the work he has started in you! Hold onto that because God has called you and already started something in you that He wants to finish in you! But don't let me get ahead of myself because we will deal with more of that a little later down the line! So, you see, you are a three-part being, and although you may or may not see with your natural eyes, you are to perceive with your spiritual ones for sure!

This next scripture speaks of our connection with God and how we, as His daughters, should desire to be with Him with every part of ourselves: spirit, soul, and body!

My soul yearns for you in the night;
in the morning my spirit longs for you...
Isaiah 26:9 (NIV)

Even Mary, the mother of Jesus, acknowledged the fact she was a three-part being! She recognized by receiving this amazing revelation who she was created to be and what she was called to do!

And Mary said, "My soul magnifies the Lord, and my
spirit rejoices in God my Savior, for he has looked on the
humble estate of his servant. For behold, from now on
all generations will call me blessed;"
Luke 1:46-48 (ESV)
(Underlined words are added by the author for emphasis.)

Through the angel that spoke to Mary, God gave her a

word that caused her to perceive, without seeing it naturally how blessed she was. She recognized everyone from many generations would speak about how God had chosen her and released the blessing over her life! Thus, she prophesied that generations after her would call her blessed!

You and I must see past our current situation to see with anticipation the very blessed position our Heavenly Father has for us to be in. Not down the line, but right now. Not in the sweet by and by like the old church used to say, but right in the current here and now! God has something for you to see, and it starts with your perception to receive what God is showing you.

JOSHUA

In the book of Joshua, after the servant of the Lord, Moses had died, Joshua had been commissioned to lead the children of Israel across the country to inhabit the expanse of land and property God had for all His people. God leads Joshua forward by encouraging him to see what the Lord was giving to him: victory over the enemy before his eyes.

And the LORD said unto Joshua, See, I have given into thine hand Jericho, and the king thereof, and the mighty men of valour.
Joshua 6:2 (KJV)

Hebrew is the original language of the Old Testament Bible. In the New Strong's Expanded Dictionary of Bible

Words: Hebrew and Greek Dictionaries, the word *see* means *to see in totality without limitations*. I love this definition! It means *to see by vision, perceive, discern, pay close attention, look intently, and gaze upon joyfully*. This is precisely the way our Heavenly Father desires for you and me to see! God doesn't just want you to see your current obstacle that may be in front of you, but with spirit-filled perception, past the right now problem, right into the victory He has for you on the other side!

Before the battle had even begun, God was causing Joshua to see, not with his natural eyes, but He caused him to perceive by vision and revelation what He was giving to him in his hand. God has something He desires, yes, desires for you to see what He has given to you, which is so close, it's right in your hand. Can you see it? Can you perceive it? It's the vision of the Lord right in front of you! He has it for you! It's yours! Take a moment to see what God the Father is eager to show you; this may take closing your eyes to see clearly.

SEEING SENSIBLY

It's also essential to see what not to do and where not to go as well. This is also vital and something I couldn't leave out.

Sensible people will see trouble coming and avoid it,
but an unthinking person will walk
right into it and regret it later.
Proverbs 22:3 (GNB)

This passage is written exactly the same way in ***Proverbs 27:12*** in this same translation with no variation. This scripture in the Book of Wisdom written twice with the same wording exemplifies how important it is to see sensibly and perceive wisely! Seeing sensibly will help you in your decision-making process because you'll be able to reason through problems as you see them clearly! Let me give it to you this way in another Bible translation. I think you'll get a kick out of it, and if you don't, hold on to this one for a while; you just might need it. This is a part of the sense realm called common sense.

When you see trouble coming, don't be stupid and walk right into it — be smart and hide.
Proverbs 22:3 (CEV)

God desires you to experience the gift of seeing with practical and spiritual vision for your life, family, future, and right now. Seeing the way your Heavenly Father desires for you to see is something you can continue to ask Him for. You do not need to be without this important commodity in your life. It's available for you to operate in right now. See now what God has given you in your hand! See what God is revealing to you in your heart for your future!

I pray that your hearts will be flooded with light so that you can see something of the future he has called you to share. I want you to realize that God has been made rich because we who are Christ's have been given to him!
Ephesians 1:18 (TLB)

This is completely amazing! God desires to give you glimpses of your future that have been crafted and designed by Him just for you. It's down the road, and as you keep walking with Him, it becomes clearer as you journey on the path the Lord has called you to.

The path of the righteous is like the morning sun,
shining ever brighter till the full light of day.
Proverbs 4:18 (NIV)

The best possible future we can have is a future shared with Him! There is no getting away from this crucial point! What an incredible realization to come to understand we have been given as a gift to God according to the previous passage of scripture in *Ephesians 1:18*! When we were introduced to our Savior Jesus Christ, Who died on the cross of Calvary thousands of years ago, and said, yes, to Him, we became a gift to our God.

As I've stated before, every person on the planet is gifted; every person on this planet has a gift. Most people operate in it in some form or another. They just can't help it; it's in them. It's how people use their gifts that becomes the problem! Not everyone realizes (sees with understanding) that it's the gift God created for His purpose, for them to be. Seeing by revelation Who God is in you reveals so much more of who you are: an amazing, very precious, very special gift! If there is a special sacrificial gift given, then that gift should be cared

111

for and cherished. Seeing yourself clearly by acknowledging the God in you causes you to cherish who you are: the gifted Leading Lady!

SEE CLEARLY

We are a cherished possession our Heavenly Father has hand-crafted with purpose, on purpose. He does not want you or me to walk in this life, a life which He has given to us to have in abundance, seeing without insight. We must see with the lens of faith. The scripture in Hebrew 11:6 says, *"Without faith it is impossible to please God."* It goes on to say, *"Those who come to God,"* which is to ask for Him and to want and desire Him, *"must believe God is,"* meaning we must believe He is Who He says He is: God the Real and Eternal God. He's the God of all Hope, the God of all Consolation! He's the God we may not see with our natural eyes, but we can perceive with our spiritual eyes!

One of His names is Jehovah Shammah, the God Who is There, and where is that? It's wherever we need Him to be! He's always right there with us! The scripture continues with this promise that God will *"Reward the faith of anyone who seeks after Him."* According to the Word of God, we must come to God in faith, and we must see everything around us through the lens of our faith-walk with God.

Again the Word of God says in 2 Corinthians 5:7, *"We walk by faith not by sight."* The sight this scripture speaks of is the everyday natural realm, which is what we see with our natural eyes. As I stated, God wants us to see Him. That's exactly what He said to Joshua *"See I."* To see clearly is to see God first.

With everything going on around us and in every situation we face, we should see Him through it all, even through the harsh reality of present problems and internal or external pain! See Him first because to see Him, to really see Him, is to see clearly!

The Lord has given us the ability to see, Leading Ladies, to see past disappointments, past the negative circumstances, and even to see beyond the superficial and temporal realm. Yes, the everyday issues we face may always be before us, and they may all be very real. I'm not negating the struggle is real, but God has so much more in store for you, and it starts by seeing clearly.

FROM BLURRY TO FOCUSED

"Seeing is a gift that comes with practice."
STEPHANIE MILLS

I was sitting outside looking at the scenery one day, but I didn't have my contacts or glasses on. Sometimes when I first get up in the morning, I don't immediately put on my glasses. I start the day moving around my house to fix breakfast, taking vitamins, and even reading without clear vision. I don't really notice everything I'm seeing is blurry and out of focus. I just get up and start doing stuff. I've allowed myself to become accustomed to the blur. The only reason I can accomplish my tasks without too much of a hindrance is because I'm familiar with my surroundings. Sometimes, when I'm not in familiar territory, I'll fumble around not being able to focus on anything clearly.

As I was sitting outside enjoying the beauty of the great outdoors, I was thinking about all kinds of things filtering around in my mind as well as meditating on God's Goodness. I looked down next to me, saw the glasses I'd been carrying around, and decided to put them on. Yep, I was carrying my glasses around with me from place to place in the case, not wearing them. Low and behold, you wouldn't believe it! Everything around me came into pristine and perfect focus; my surroundings became clear and illuminated!

When I looked around, I could make out the qualities of everything I saw with precision! Nothing was a blur anymore! I had the audacity to be amazed at the difference in my vision! The clarity in what was right in front of me and all around me was shocking! I had been going around for most of the morning, as usual, not seeing clearly at all! I had even become accustomed to operating this way for a part of each day. Trying to accomplish all these tasks without the ability to see precisely what I was doing had become a common occurrence throughout my mornings.

As soon as I put my glasses on, bringing everything around me into complete focus, the Lord spoke to me so clearly right at that moment. He said, *"This is how I want you to see all that I want to show you in the natural realm, in the spirit realm and the things I have for you in your future. This is the way I desire My Word to be to you when you read it. I want it to be clear, precise, and unquestionable in understanding what I'm revealing, what I'm saying, and what I'm showing."* Wow, it was almost like when I was able to see clearly, I could hear clearly! To be honest, the Words the Lord spoke to me that day were much fewer, but this is what was revealed to me or rather the impression I received as I sat and meditated on what He actually spoke!

*"If you go as far as you can see,
you will then see enough to go even farther."*
JOHN WOODEN

This clear vision and hearing takes you lending your life
to the Lord. For example, the Bible talks about a priest of
the Lord serving in the temple of God, who'd begun to lose
his sight. The Bible says that while Eli was the priest of the
Lord, there was no open vision, and the Word of the Lord was
rare (1 Samuel 3:1-3). His lack of vision (not just physically
but most importantly spiritually) did not just affect him, but
because of his position, it affected the entire nation of Israel.

Whatever position or place you have in life, it's important
for you to see clearly for you and for those connected to
you. You cannot afford to allow your familiarity with your
surroundings to cause you to go through the motions doing
the same thing every day without really seeing what you're
doing or focusing on what's in front of you. For example, most
car accidents happen close to where people live just because
they are familiar with their surroundings and don't pay close
attention to where they are going or what they're doing. Don't
take for granted you know what's in front of you because you
see it and experience it every day. Always take the time to pay
attention; God might want to show you something different,
which may cause you to hear something special.

Seeing with the eyes of faith in your Heavenly Father is
the epitome of perception. Everything around you can literally
be completely going catawampus! Yet, through it all, you can
see the victory right on the other side of it as you perceive with

understanding what God is showing you. The Leading Lady sees clearly because of her closeness with the Lord.

CHAPTER 6

Qualities Of The Leading Lady

"Words have incredible power.
They can make people's hearts soar,
or they can make people's hearts sore."
DR. MARCY GROTHE

THE LEADING LADY SPEAKS

"Your speech betrays you." This is what the witnesses exclaimed to Peter during the trial of Jesus Christ. And yes, this is the Peter who is one of the 12 apostles of the Lamb; the same Peter whose name will be written on one of the 12 gates in the New Jerusalem (Rev. 21:14). He is the very Peter who preached to crowds of thousands to be converted to Christ as shared in the book of Acts, which is the Acts of the Apostles.

Yes, this Peter has a story!

117

Peter, one of the disciples of Jesus Christ at the time, was sitting in a courtyard watching the trial proceedings of all ages. The Bible says a young lady, seeing Peter, calls out to him, *"Hey, you're one of Jesus' followers, aren't you?"* Peter denies the accusation saying that he didn't know Him. Then, as Peter began to walk away, another said, *"Yep, I'm pretty sure that you were one of the ones that were with him."* Again, Peter became upset and told them he doesn't know what they're talking about. But then another confirms, *"I know you were with him because your speech indeed gives you away."*

When Peter opened his mouth to speak, his speech gave away the fact that he had been with Jesus. Just by the way Peter spoke, it was evident that he had been hanging out with the Lord. Can you imagine? Peter's lingo gave away that he walked with Jesus, talked with Jesus, and had a relationship with Jesus; therefore, Peter sounded just like Jesus. To change his speech, he began cursing, making sure to disassociate himself from the Savior of the world, vehemently denying his connection with Him.

Just as Jesus predicted when they had their last supper together, Peter denied the Lord three times before the night was over. Peter, of course, was undoubtedly ashamed of his actions and wept bitterly. Yet, as we read through later discourse and Jesus' unrelenting love, we discover that he is converted back to God and serves Him faithfully throughout his lifetime!

Depending on who or what you're around the most, you'll begin to sound like your surroundings. Your association influences your speech. You'll have the same dialect of the people and culture, which is what gave Peter away. You will act and sound like what you've been immersed in. What you say is in direct correlation to what you've heard, what you've learned, what you believe, and what you perceive to be right and true. Your speech is entrenched in what you've allowed into your psyche, and ultimately what you've allowed in your heart. Apostle Holcomb often said, *"What's in your heart abundantly will come out of your mouth eventually."*

...For out of the abundance of the heart the mouth speaks.
Matthew 12:34 (NKJV)

The real examination to correct your speech takes place in the heart. What is in your heart that causes you to speak the way you do? What do you sound like when you speak? What does your speech give away about you? What are the words you use that may associate you with a certain place or situation or certain person? Words have meaning, and words hold value. What you speak says quite a bit about you. Does your speech give away that you've been with the Lord?

A LEARNED SKILL

The beautiful thing about learning to speak the right words is just that: speaking right is a learned skill. As Job said in Job 6:25, *"How forcible are right words!"* The right words hold a force and have force behind them that, when learned, can be a gift and an amazing tool in your life and the lives of those you influence! The right words are everything, and we can study to speak the right kind of words, especially if you put your heart into it! The Word of God tells us that we can actually learn what to speak by studying how to answer.

The heart of the righteous studies how to answer, But the mouth of the wicked pours forth evil.
Proverbs 15:28 (NKJV)

The only way evil words can easily be poured out of any person is because those words are poured into that person. It's what they may have learned and internalized over time. The only way negative, hurtful, and harmful words are released from someone's mouth is for that same reason; these words are in their heart. We can change our hearts by studying what we are always going to say. This is the goal of the Leading Lady, and as I keep declaring, that my dear is you!

When she speaks, her words are wise, and kindness is the rule for everything she says.
Proverbs 31:26 (TLB)

As a Leading Lady in your own right and in your realm, your words are weighty; they can add value to others or tear down those around you. Sometimes, we don't consider our words when we speak, but we should. Our words hold power and have power; what we say matters. I know sometimes we may believe that the weight of our words may not be significant to others with whom we engage, but, on the contrary, our words hold a lasting effect on the hearer.

Has someone said something to you that either encouraged you or burdened you? You may have thought, *"Well, that person doesn't even really matter to me,"* yet their words held you captive, perhaps only for a moment, maybe even longer. Either way, those words produced something in you. With those words spoken to you, you either need to pluck them up out of your mind or, if they were words of praise, encouragement, compassion, or even correction, you should internalize them and allow the words to push you further. I'll write it again: words affect all of us.

We all know this nursery rhyme, or I may be dating myself with this, but it says, *"Sticks and stones may break my bones, but words will never hurt me."* The only reason I'm sure this nursery rhyme was written is because words do hurt. My interpretation is that the writer was trying to encourage the reader or the hearer of the rhyme that, although some words can hurt on the onset, we can shake them off and not allow them to hurt for long.

Words are precious, and words are powerful, but words don't have to be permanent. We get to choose for ourselves which words stick and stay and which words to reject and give away.

My daughter Brittney teaches kindergarten. She's constantly having to encourage the children, while correcting them, to use the right words to express themselves and not use words with their classmates that would hurt and harm. One instance she shared with me involved two little girls who

played together every day; they even called each other best
friends. Now, how much interaction they had outside of the
classroom setting was probably little to none, but in school,
they were true confidants, bosom buddies, allies in arms!

One day, these two little girls were playing outside for
recess, and due to some disagreement or another, one little girl
told the other her hair was ugly! Oh, horror of horrors, the
little girl who heard these words was mortified and ran crying
to her teacher, screaming, *"Ms.Giddens! Ms.Giddens! Little so
and so said my hair was ugly!"* This little girl's best friend in all
the world said something hurtful and horrible! What was Ms.
Giddens to do? She bent right down to the little girl's level, and
instead of telling her, *"Your hair isn't ugly; your hair is very pretty,"*
Ms. Giddens knew the words already spoken had done their
damage. Instead of contradicting the negative words released
into the atmosphere, Ms. Giddens asked her a question,
"Well, is your hair ugly?" The little girl replied, *"No."* Then she
responded to this little girl, *"Well, then you can't listen to her when
she told you your hair is ugly."* The little girl responded, *"But she's
my best friend!"*

After a few more words of encouragement and speaking
to the other little girl about kindness and speaking the right
words, the two little girls' worlds were turned back right side
up! Ms. Giddens saved the day, until the next incident, of
course. I know that may seem a bit trivial to our adult minds,
and the reaction of these children is extreme in this case, but
the point is, words are effective to do just what we send them
out of our mouths to do. And depending on the relationship
we have with the person we're speaking to, the effect can be
devastating, or at least hurtful and not helpful. On the other

hand, the words that we speak can bring help and healing to the soul; it depends on how we use our words.

> *Think twice before you speak,*
> *because your words and influence will plant the seed*
> *of either success or failure in the mind of another.*
> NAPOLEON HILL

It's said that "actions speak louder than words." Actions do indeed solidify words more strongly. But words help actions to be understood. For example, I read a love story where the male character expressed his love to the heroine in different ways, but she was still confused about his feelings because he never said, *"I love you."* As the story went on, she tried to just accept that, although he never gave her the words, she believed that indeed she was loved.

As time went on, things got tough as things in life often do, and she realized that she needed those words. Finally, there was a break-up, you know drama, as with any story, good or bad, there's always drama. The young man was upset because things weren't going right with his lady love. He spoke to his mother about the problems affecting their relationship, and his mother hit him upside the head and told him, *"Give her the words!"* Actions are very important, for sure, but sometimes we still need "the words."

WORDS: ASSET OR LIABILITY

The Living Bible version of Proverbs 31:26 says, *"When she speaks her words are wise, and kindness is the rule for everything she says."* This means before this Leading Lady speaks, she's aware that her words are influential, and the hearer values her words; she makes sure she abides by certain rules: the rule to speak with wisdom and also the rule to use kindness. We should measure our words when we speak. What is the rule of your tongue?

And so the tongue is a small part of the body yet it carries great power! Just think of how a small flame can set a huge forest ablaze. And the tongue is a fire! It can be compared to the sum total of wickedness and is the most dangerous part of our human body. It corrupts the entire body and is a hellish flame! It releases a fire that can burn throughout the course of human existence. For every wild animal on earth including birds, creeping reptiles, and creatures of the sea and land have all been overpowered and tamed by humans, but the tongue is not able to be tamed. It's a fickle, unrestrained evil that spews out words full of toxic poison! We use our tongue to praise God our Father and then turn around and curse a person who was made in his very image! Out of the same mouth we pour out words of praise one minute and curses the next. My brothers and sisters, this should never be!
James 3:5-10 TPT

Leading Lady, we must be careful of the things our tongues release because it is indeed being used to release something in your life and the lives of those around you! Our tongues hold power!

---

*Your words are so powerful that they will kill or give
life, and the talkative person will reap the consequences.*
Proverbs 18:21 TPT

Your words can be weapons of mass destruction! If used
lethally to cause harm, it can lead to an avalanche of upheaval
and deep scars that can be very difficult to heal and overcome,
even when the wounding words are unintentionally spoken.
However, your words, Leading Lady, are meant to heal and
help, build and bridge, so those who listen to you do better, go
further, reach higher and live longer just because you speak!

---

*Sharing words of wisdom is satisfying to
your inner being. It encourages you to know
that you've changed someone else's life.*
Proverbs 18:20 TPT

The Leading Lady in you is a woman of wisdom when
you allow yourself to develop, grow, and mature. Wisdom is
the thing that's in you that you must speak out of your mouth
to those God has given you to influence! This is how you're
satisfied—by speaking words of wisdom!

There is a quote that says, *"Those who live by the sword die
by the sword."* This saying is loosely based on scripture. Yet,
you will live or die by the words of your mouth! Mentally,

emotionally, spiritually, and physically, we will live or die by the words we release from our mouths. You can speak your way into a fulfilling life, or you can cut your life short by continuing to let negative speech flow from your lips.

This "theory," if you would, is not only biblically sound; it is even used in the economic and business world. There are many articles and books written about the power of your speech and how, through the right teaching, what you release continually from your mouth can change your world. You can speak your way into good physical health, a new business, change for your future, and stability in your life. When you speak with positive words of affirmation to those around you to bring an increase to their life and yours, you're changing your world by your words! This is the example of our Heavenly Father; He spoke the world into existence (Genesis 1), and He has given us the power in our mouths to do the same!

Respond gently when you are confronted and you'll defuse the rage of another. Responding with sharp, cutting words will only make it worse. Don't you know that being angry can ruin the testimony of even the wisest of men (or women)? When wisdom speaks, understanding becomes attractive. But the words of the fool make their ignorance look laughable.
Proverbs 15:1-2 TPT

(Words in parentheses added by the author for emphasis.)

Can you imagine? The verbiage you use when you speak can make the words you say become attractive! Taking the time to respond with the right words in any and every situation is extremely important. We have the ability to do just that as wise women of God which is who you are, so go ahead and say so. It takes humility to respond gently in a hostile confrontation. Yet, with inner strength and confidence in who you are and the Help of God's Holy Spirit, you can do it! Let me reiterate this point: words hold power! Your words have the power to close doors or unlock countless blessings for yourself! That is why it's always vital to choose "right words!"

We cannot constantly use our mouths to complain and speak forth negative words and then try to use the same mouth to release God's blessings. Therefore, with the mighty weapon of your tongue instead of the former, release the blessing of the Lord over yourself, your household, and others as well.

We must tame the tongue and rule our world!

THE LEADING LADY STANDS

"Be sure you put your feet
in the right place, then stand firm."
ABRAHAM LINCOLN

"Stand still and see the salvation of the Lord." These are Moses' words to the children of Israel as they watched with complete dismay the Egyptian army coming toward them full speed in chariots and horses. They were standing but scared. They were standing with their loved ones and possessions in their arms with nowhere to run because the Red Sea was in front with the enemy coming up fast behind them!

The children of Israel didn't realize they were standing

on the brink of a miracle. I'm sure they thought they were standing, waiting for the end of their lives right in the middle of an unknown desert place. They didn't recognize God had a miracle on His Mind for His people. Even their leader Moses was scared, praying fervently for God to do something even as he spoke aloud to all those who had followed him out into that wilderness place.

And oh, did God do something alright! They stood there and watched as He lifted the waters off the ground and parted the way for the children of Israel to cross over on dry ground! And then, if that wasn't enough, He caused those same soldiers along with their Pharaoh to be completely destroyed by the same waters that the children of Israel walked through! Then, after all was said and done, they stood there on the other side of the sea and watched their enemy swept away!

As I've stated before, we are the people of God, and we are not standing without the full strength of God's Goodness on our side. When we stand in faith, standing assured on the Word of God, we are not standing helpless like the children of Israel thought they were. We are standing right on the brink of seeing God work things out for our good!

Therefore put on the full armor of God, so that when the day of evil comes, you may be able to stand your ground, and after you have done everything, to stand. Stand firm...
Ephesians 6:13-14 (NIV)

The Leading Lady stands firm on the Word of God! That's the entire reason we can stand strong. The strength is in the Power of His unchanging Word! I love Moses' stance. First, he yells out to the millions of Jews standing in the middle of what looks like a complete and utter disaster and tells them to *"Stand still and see what God is going to do to get us out of this mess!"* Then, he turns to God and prays, *"God, how in the world are you going to get us out of this mess?!"*

Sometimes, that's just how you must stand! You may wiggle and wobble, but you won't fall down! At least you won't be down for long because you can get right back up again! And you won't be knocked down for long either because you're taking the stand and standing strong! Standing your ground, believing God is going to get you out of the mess. Standing firm, declaring by speaking out loud that God is going to get you through this test! Standing, knowing that when the evil day comes, your stance is solid, and the promise of God's Word is sure!

Standing seeing by faith, even what's not available to see in the natural realm, what God was planning for you all along! God just might part that problem right down the middle and allow you to walk straight through it! Standing with strength because the Greater One that's on the inside of you is standing as well (1 John 4:4)! Oh, glory! That's enough of a reason to run around the space that you're in right now because you're not alone in your strong stance; you've got Someone much stronger standing with you because He's in you! I love what the Message Bible translation says about getting back up again!

*Don't interfere with good people's lives; don't try
to get the best of them. No matter how many times
you trip them up, God-loyal people don't
stay down long; Soon they're up on their feet,
while the wicked end up flat on their faces.*
Proverbs 24:15-16 (MSG)

When the enemy interferes with you, which is what he's known to do, you won't stay down for long. So don't keep yourself down when the word says you should be getting right back up on your feet! Standing!

The scriptures in Ephesians 6 states that when you're covered with God's full armor, which is all centered in God's Word, you can stand against every single wicked thing the enemy tries to bring against you. This scripture is empowering because it says that you can still stand when you've done everything you know to do. If you weren't capable of standing strong and standing firm, then your Bible wouldn't say that "Yes, you can stand!" So, when all that's within you wants to quit and stay down, remember you have greatness in you, saying, "Go ahead and get back up and stand!"

*And that about wraps it up. God is strong, and he wants
you strong. So take everything the Master has set
out for you, well-made weapons of the best materials.*

And put them to use so you will be able to stand up to
everything the Devil throws your way.
Ephesians 6:10-11 (MSG)

You can do this! You can stand strong, and you can stand long. You've got all of Heaven backing you up and holding you up when you're standing still right on the firm foundation of the Word of God! *The Leading Lady Stands* because she can. You, my dear beautiful lady, most definitely can!

LEADING LADY FOR CHANGE

"A leader takes people where they want to go.
A great leader takes people where they don't
necessarily want to go, but ought to be."
ROSALYNN CARTER

Before we go to the next chapter, I'd like to interrupt by inserting another Leading Lady from our American history. I left off with encouragement about *The Leading Lady Stands.* Well, this Leading Lady stood up for so many amazing causes! She was the First Lady of the United States from 1933 to 1945. Anna Eleanor Roosevelt was the longest-serving First Lady throughout her husband, President Franklin D. Roosevelt's four terms in office. She was an American politician, diplomat, and activist who later served as a United Nations spokeswoman, and she was a revolutionary during her time!

She was an early champion of civil rights for African Americans as well as an advocate for American workers, the poor, young people, and women during the Great Depression. She also supported government-funded programs for artists and writers.

In 1933, Mrs. Roosevelt became the first First Lady to hold her own press conference. In an attempt to afford equal time to women, who were traditionally barred from presidential press conferences, she in turn only allowed female reporters to attend.

She wrote her own news articles, chronicling political policies and issues along with her own life in office, in a publication called *The Day*. She also authored over 27 books, including her own biography. After her husband became paralyzed during his tenure as President of the United States from poliomyelitis, she became his eyes and ears.

Eleanor Roosevelt, as First Lady, drove across the nation by herself, visiting the Japanese internment camps, coal miners, and other disenfranchised people throughout the nation, getting to know them to somehow aid in an attempt to bring awareness and help. She never stopped her efforts to aid and assist people of all ethnicities and cultures, not only in the United States but all over the world, even after leaving the White House.

Wherever and whenever she could be an influence for change, hope and help, she was. I just wanted to take a moment to highlight this Leading Lady in history. It is written of her that she never thought much of herself, but she began to see where there was so much need in so many areas, so she used her platform to encourage change. Not everything she did turned out successfully; some things failed miserably, but she got out there and did what she could and became a pretty awesome icon in her day!

"Life is what you make it.
Always has been, always will be."
ELEANOR ROOSEVELT

"A woman is like a tea bag; you never know
how strong it is until it's in hot water."
ELEANOR ROOSEVELT

As we turn the page, let's move on to our next three characteristics!

Dr. Halene Giddens

CHAPTER 7

Characteristics Of The Leading Lady

THE LEADING LADY SURRENDERS

*"Sometimes, it's not the times you decide to fight,
but the times you decide to surrender,
that makes all the difference."*
SISSY GAVRILAKI

"I Surrender." With both hands lifted high above our heads, this should be the very words we speak and the position we take every day. Every morning when you wake up with the brand-new gift of today, just lift both arms and hands way up in the air and say, *"I Surrender."* Everything we have and all that we are should be given over to our God: mind, body, and soul! It must be a daily confession that we make. The reason being is that we tend to take back what we should continually give to

135

Him, which is ourselves.

Surrender your heart to God, turn to him in prayer, and
give up your sins —even those you do in secret. Then you
won't be ashamed; you will be confident and fearless.
Job 11:13-15 (CEV)

Living life in surrender to God is not a sign of weakness but a true indication of strength. Surrendering your heart to God leads to a life of confidence and fearlessness with Him. You can take heart in knowing everything you are and desire to be has been turned over in surrender to your God. According to the American Heritage Dictionary, surrender means *to yield (something) to the possession or power of another*. This is exactly what we do when we give ourselves up to God. It's not an easy endeavor because we like to be in charge of our own destiny and fate. We have a need to be in the driver's seat. We don't like being out of control or feeling as though we're out of control; it is not comfortable. It is sometimes painstakingly difficult for all of us!

> *"The moment of surrender is not when life is over,*
> *it's when it begins."*
> MARIANNE WILLIAMSON

This giving of ourselves completely to God is a total mind alteration, a paradigm shift to everything we read and hear in the age we live in right now! It's geometrically opposed to the "world's" way of thinking. Due to the abuse of power from those in places of position over the years, whether we've been on the receiving end of it or have heard about or have seen the abuse of authority, words like surrender and submission make people cringe; well, I mean most women. Instead, these two words should bring us to a place of solace and peace instead of anxiety and stress! If we know our "place," which should be a place of peace and protection to bring about our perfection, then this place of surrender would be embraced joyfully. God's perfect place of surrender leads us to the perfect place of peace with Him: positioned right in the pocket of where we need to be in the perfect timeframe of when we need to be there!

But I trust in you, LORD; I say, "You are my God."
My times are in your hands;...
Psalms 31:14-15 a portion (NIV)

The starting of anything new can be exhilarating and exciting as well as fill you with apprehension and stress; sometimes it's just plain scary. A friend of ours used to say something to me that is so apropos for where we as sons and daughters of God need to be. He's since gone on to be with the Lord, yet his voice still sounds in my ear. When he and his wife first started their church, he would say, looking up towards heaven, "Look, God. No hands!" When he looked around and saw what God was doing through the ministry He committed to their care, he would say, "God is actually doing this without my help."

It's not that they weren't working and handling the ministry of the Lord, but instead of working for the Lord, they allowed the Lord to work through them. They had to surrender and say, I'm taking my hands off, and God, You keep your Hands of Guidance on. It's like learning how to ride a bike; once you really learn how to pedal and keep the wheels steady, you can sometimes take your hands off the handlebars and go! Well, when you get that comfortable, you can lift your hands and say, "Look, Dad, no hands!" That's trust in your ability to ride a bike!

I must admit I never took my hands off the handlebars when I was a young girl riding my bicycle. I was never that confident in my bike-riding skills. My friends and I rode our bikes all over town and much farther from place to place, visiting all of our friends everywhere we could, as far as we could go! Bike-riding was so much fun! We'd be gone for hours, almost every day, riding our bikes, downhill, uphill as fast as we could, and I always kept my hands, albeit sometimes loosely, on those handlebars. It didn't matter how many summers I'd been riding or how comfortable I'd become riding my bicycle; some part of my hands were always kept on the handlebars.

That is usually the way we surrender to God. We've got one hand up and one on the handlebars. Even if it's a loose hold, we still have our hands right there holding on. It's that feeling of always remaining in control, even a little bit, just in case something goes wrong. We may even take our hands off for a moment, but if things look and feel a little shaky, we grab those bars in a tight grip with both hands. But a person relying upon their riding ability—someone who's been cycling for a long time—will ride that ten-speed, eight-speed, beach cruiser, or whatever it is with their hands folded across their chest looking straight ahead, relaxed and comfortable on that bicycle. That's trust in their own expertise of being able to handle their bike with ease.

Our Heavenly Father has expertise as well, and He can handle our lives with ease, along with everything that surrounds our lives and every single thing that concerns us. This includes your family, finances, future, and your faith; He can handle it all! You'd be surprised what God can do without your meddling hands mingling in His perfect pocket of a plan for you. Surrender it all to Him; you don't have to be in the driver's seat of your life; you don't have to hold the purse strings for your future. The Lord knows how to guide you in every decision you make along with every step you take. All it takes for you and me is surrender, looking up to Heaven with our eyes on Him. The best way to experience His expertise in the handling of our lives is for us to take our hands off, lift our hands up and say, "Look, Father, no hands."

THE LEADING LADY SACRIFICES

*"You can't achieve anything in life
without a small amount of sacrifice."*
SHAKIRA

Sacrifice is another word we really don't like to hear, see, or use. I'm not sure it's even in our English vernacular in the day and time we're living in! Yet, people are still doing it; everyone sacrifices something to get something else—it's inevitable. So, the question is: what is your sacrifice?

> *"You are not happy with any sacrifice. Otherwise, I would offer one to you. You are not pleased with burnt offerings. The sacrifice pleasing to God is a broken spirit. O God, you do not despise a broken and sorrowful heart. Then you will be pleased with sacrifices offered in the right spirit—"*
> Psalms 51:16-17, 19 GW

Living a life of sacrifice to God is part of the Christian experience, or at least it should be. It should be a part of the life of any God-inspired Leading Lady. It's not a negative, but a positive. If you have children, you do everything you can for them to set them up for an abundant future; this is the will of God to be able to do just that (Proverbs 13:22; Psalm 37:25,26). If you've gone after a career, learning to become skilled in that profession takes sacrifice. In that regard, you give to get. You give your time and money to receive a better education to get the job that hopefully pays more.

If you're going to be the best in whatever you pursue, then you've got to give your best. There's nothing wrong with walking in this thing called sacrifice, especially when you look at how sacrifice benefits you in the end. As I stated, we're all sacrificing something in our lives, so what are you making these sacrifices for? What is your ultimate goal in doing it? We understand that some live a life of sacrifice for their families, career, and sometimes friends and others. But the highest level of sacrifice, the most important sacrifice, is first and foremost to our God.

140

Everything we do in living this life to be pleasing to our God is offered to Him as a sacrifice! The beautiful thing about offering ourselves sacrificially to God is He then becomes pleasing to you and me! (1 John 3:22, 1 Chronicles 17:26-27). Of course, we know Jesus Christ has already given the ultimate sacrifice by laying His life down for you and me. He gave Himself to receive all of us, along with any and everyone else who would say "yes" to Him! He gave to get! We now, in turn, give ourselves in sacrifice to get more intimate knowledge of Him (Proverbs 8:17).

Offer right sacrifices,
and put your trust in the LORD.
Psalms 4:5 (ESV)

We are the right sacrifice given over to God as we trust Him completely. That's what Surrender is, that's what Sacrifice is, and that's what Submission is—complete reliance on our Savior. The only way and reason we can do these three things is if we trust Him. That's the ultimate sacrifice, the giving of ourselves, trusting Him fully!

Here's the backdrop of Psalm chapter 51, an entire prayer of repentance written by David, the king God set over His people, Israel. David sinned against God by sleeping with Bathsheba—another man's wife—after looking across his balcony and seeing her bathing outside on her own balcony! Now, you may think this is a bit racy: bathing outside in the middle of the day nude. But, remember, all the men were supposed to be at war, including the king, who decided to chill at the house instead.

The narrative says this was the time "kings went to war." So, David should have had himself right there on the battlefield with his men! And if that wasn't enough, Bathsheba becomes pregnant by David, so he decides to bring Uriah, her husband, home from the war! He can do that because, as you know, he's the king! David brings Uriah back home to sleep with his wife to cover up the infidelity! Uriah wouldn't sleep with Bathsheba even after David, mind you, got him drunk. Uriah understood that it was the time of war and not a time of communing with his beautiful wife! His brethren were out fighting for the nation of Israel against the Philistines, and that is where Uriah knew he needed to be. So, he slept on the palace steps, King David's home, and wouldn't go to his own home to be with his wife!

King David doesn't stop there! He sends Uriah, a faithful servant to David, back to the battlefield, where David instructs Joab, his head general and nephew, to make sure Uriah is killed in battle! After all of this, David brings Bathsheba back to the castle to become his new queen! I know, right—this is craziness! Whelp, here comes the prophet Nathan to say, "Bruh, what in the world are you doing?" Okay, he didn't really say it that way. He actually told David a story about a man who had anything and everything he ever thought he wanted, but then he took the only thing another man possessed and had that man killed for it! David was outraged—go figure—and said, "This man should be throttled or killed or something!" Nathan paused, looked King David in the eye, and said, "Dude, you're the man!" After hearing what Nathan spoke to him, David was completely broken in his heart by all that he had done.

In the midst of this, Bathsheba gives birth to David's son. This first child dies after several days of him praying and fasting for the baby, although David knew the baby's death was a part of God's judgment against him. After all of this, David finally begins to pour his heart out to God in repentance, and in this part of Psalm 51, he talks about the sacrifice God wants. He says, "God, you're not pleased with just any sacrifice, or else I'd give that to You! Instead, what You require is for me to be broken before You. You desire for my heart and spirit to become contrite so that You can heal and help me with Your forgiving grace and love. You, Father, desire my heart first and foremost."

David continues and says, "Then You will accept my sacrificial offerings that I give from my hands." What is so incredible about all of this is that God is so willing and ready to forgive us of anything and everything if we would simply come to Him, laying ourselves down as the sacrifice. Their second child together, Solomon, grows up to become the chosen heir to David's throne.

Our Heavenly Father is willing to heal us of our past hurts, our past mistakes, and especially of the past wounds that someone else committed against us! We've got to lay it all down as a sacrificial burnt offering to our God. We must lay ourselves down before Him in humility, knowing that we can't do anything without Him. (John 15:5)! This sacrificial life begins by allowing ourselves to be completely broken before God (Matthew 21:44 Luke 20:18). It's the complete sacrifice of our hearts; it's the contrition of our spirits. So then sacrifice starts with the heart and then gives with the hands.

Our supreme sacrifice is to our amazing God; it's always a matter of our heart towards Him: I am so grateful to know that even when our behavior is unacceptable, it doesn't mean we are unforgivable. God's ability to love and forgive us despite our displeasing actions is what makes His Grace so amazing and His Love so incredible.

Abraham gave what's known as an extreme sacrifice to his God. Abraham, the patriarch in the Old Testament scriptures, went to sacrifice his son Isaac on the altar on Mount Moriah after God asked him to do so. God said, "Take your son Isaac, your only son, go to the land of Moriah and give him as a burnt offering to me." Can you imagine God asking Abraham to give up his only son! We know Abraham had another son named Ishmael, who he conceived with an Egyptian woman named Hagar, his wife Sarah's handmaiden.

By the way, this was all Sarah's idea; I mentioned this situation in one of the previous chapters. I know Abraham could've said "no," but he didn't. He desperately wanted an heir born to him; he was willing to do whatever it took to accomplish that purpose. He believed like Sarah believed that maybe this is what God meant. Hagar did become pregnant with a son, but this was not what God intended for Abraham and Sarah. Therefore, Ishmael was not the promised son; although God did bless Ishmael because he was a part of Abraham's family, he would receive a portion of the blessing of Abraham.

Isaac was the son he and his wife, Sarah, believed for all

their adult life. The son God promised to them so many years prior. Isaac is the son Sarah had given birth to in her old age. Of all the things God could've asked Abraham for, this is what God wanted? How could a God who's supposed to be a loving, caring, sharing Heavenly Father ask for something so impossible? So huge! That's like asking for everything! I love what Abraham said on the day he, his son, and his servants went up to the mountain.

"He said to his servants, 'Stay here with the donkey.
I will take the boy and we will go over there.
We will worship God in that place
and then we will come back to you.'"
Genesis 22:5 EASY

Abraham had such a trust in God that he was persuaded that if he had to sacrifice his son to God, he most definitely would! With that same persuasion in God, Abraham believed he would receive Isaac back to him! His sacrifice was an act of his worship. He said, "I and the lad will go a little farther to that place and worship, then we will return back to you." What a statement of faith! He was persuaded God would undoubtedly give him back what he had sacrificed to Him.

He knew that giving God the ultimate sacrifice, his child, was the most difficult thing he'd ever have to do! I say his *children* because he had to allow Ishmael to leave with his mother, Hagar, and there is no record of Abraham ever seeing his firstborn son, whom he also loved dearly, again. So, Abraham was well acquainted with sacrificial giving. He is the one who gave the first tenth of everything he had in his possession to God. This was long before the Mosaic Law.

---

*...and Melchizedek, the king of Salem (Jerusalem),
who was a priest of the God of Highest Heaven,
brought him bread and wine. Then Melchizedek
blessed Abram with this blessing: "The blessing of the
supreme God, Creator of heaven and earth,
be upon you, Abram; and blessed be God, who has
delivered your enemies over to you." Then Abram gave
Melchizedek a tenth of all the loot.*
Genesis 14:18-20 (TLB)

This giving of the tithe from everything he received took place after Abraham came back from a long battle against the kings of that land. These different kings from all across the countryside were fighting over territory. In the process, they had taken captive his nephew Lot and his family from the land of Sodom where they resided. Abraham wasn't even a part of this huge battle against the different kingdoms! But after hearing about his nephew's plight, he took 318 of his own trained servants to fight in this battle of nations that had come against each other.

Through all of this, Abraham 'recovered' everything that had been stolen and received all of the 'goods and bounty' just because of his efforts to rescue his nephew and family and bring them back to safety. The king of Sodom and the other kings with him were standing in gratitude for what Abraham accomplished and wanted to give him everything he had brought back. Abraham's reply was, "I won't take anything but what my young men have already eaten unless you say and tell others you have made me rich." God had already made Abraham rich; how do you think he was able to assemble 318 servants from his household? The others had to stay behind and protect all that was left! God was already doing it for Abraham because of his faithfulness to serve Him. Abraham wasn't perfect, but he was faithful.

Again, we are the living sacrifice that God desires. Nothing less will do. All He wants is you! Then everything else we have that He's given to us first, we can easily give it as a sacrifice right back to Him!

"Beloved friends, what should be our proper response to God's marvelous mercies? To surrender yourselves to God to be his sacred, living sacrifices. And live in holiness, experiencing all that delights his heart. For this becomes your genuine expression of worship."
Romans 12:1 (TPT)

The word *sacrifice* in Greek is ***thysia***. It means ***to offer up*** by fire. Of course, we're not burning our physical selves on an altar of wood like Abraham was so very much willing to do with his son Isaac. Instead, we are sacrificing ourselves, our entire being, as a gift given to our Heavenly Father, a gift we give willingly out of a heart of love toward our God. This is where sacrifice begins: out of a place of love.

When we sacrifice for our families or friends, it's out of a place of sincere love. Love is the real reason we're able to do it. That's what makes it easy, that's what makes it pleasing, and that's what makes it pure. We were created to be an expression of God's love to the world. First, it was through Jesus Christ, and now it's through each one of us who says 'yes.' This must start by laying our lives down before Him, and that's what it takes to live this sacrificial life. So, go ahead and say 'yes' to Him; not only will God be pleased, but you will be pleased as well!

THE LEADING LADY SUBMITS

Submission. Oh, boy, another tough one! Ok, let's dig in.

Usually, we look at submission in the context of wives submitting to their husbands, and yes, that is a part of it, but it's not the only part. Oh, but wait just a minute! You won't believe what I read recently; someone posted on a social media outlet saying if a girlfriend can't submit to her boyfriend, she surely won't submit to her husband. Let me tell you what I know to be so: that is a lie if I've ever seen one! Nowhere in scripture does it say girlfriend submit to your boyfriend! Nowhere! Not even in the books they left out of the Bible!

We cannot use the Word of God to make up whatever we want to fit our fancy! It does not work that way! The laying down of one's life for another and submitting one's life to the other is under a binding contract that two willing participants agree upon! This contract should not be entered into lightly! It should be entered into prayerfully, thoughtfully, carefully, and sincerely, meaning not hiding and holding things back that may be detrimental to the relationship! I don't mean talking about all the past stuff you did! Leave that stuff in the past and stop letting it affect your future.

The marital contract should be entered into openly, meaning the two parties need to be open and honest with each other! It should be entered meaningfully; your intentions are to have each other's best interest at the heart of it. He means to be a blessing to you, and you mean to be a help to him! And really mean it! It also should be entered into hopefully, to bring out the best in each other. Hoping to have the best of times with each other even when it's the worst of times, we go through it together!

It should be entered into thoughtfully with laid out goals and dreams for the future and the present. We agree upon goals and dreams even if those goals and dreams begin to develop, grow, and change along the way because sometimes they do! And at the heart of every matter, we still have each other, forever! Submission is not just something that you haphazardly give to anyone; it's contractual as well as consensual, with certain conditions and requirements that must be met. This is in every aspect and situation!

Submission is not an agreement because you're not always going to agree. Individuals see things differently, experience things differently, feel things differently; that's why we're called individuals. We all have our own thought processes, reasonings, and ways of doing things. That is why it takes great strength to submit your individually made self to someone else. Submission is bending to the one, lending to the one and giving to the one you've committed to, allowing that one to have the final decision whether you agree or not!

When you submit to someone who has your best interest at heart, always, every time, all the time, whether you like the decision or not, it's for the betterment of you both, the family, your future, your present, your purpose, your goals. So it's always what's best for the team, the two participants in this marital relationship, who've signed this marital contract and agreed to the condition and terms thereof!

You've agreed to walk this out and work it out together; it's a joint effort. Sometimes, it's about what's best for your joint endeavor, whether in ministry, business, or building your beautiful family! You're in it together! It's not a competition against one another. It's not about pitting one against the other! Your spouse is not your enemy! Your martial companion is not the one you should be up against or fighting! He's supposed to be your friend, confidant, or ride or die! He's supposed to be your ride and live because you're breathing life into each other, not sucking the life out of each other!

If one makes more money, receives more recognition, the team makes more money and receives recognition! Not that there won't be ups and downs. One may work harder than the other sometimes, and at other times the other may feel like they're doing most if not all of the work. It's a give and take; it's a back and forth. It's both parties operating in their particular strengths in the relationship to make it all come together and work! That's part of how submission works in the marriage covenant.

Alright, I got stirred up for a moment; let me bring it back down and begin at the beginning place of submission. Know that as we go on, all of what you've read is true and should be adapted into your thought process as you ponder this act of submission. Whether you're married or planning to be married in the future and even if you never plan to marry, to know is to grow. Ok, let's start at the starting place of submission: our submission to our God.

So submit yourselves to the one true God and fight against the devil and his schemes. If you do, he (the enemy) *will run away in failure. Come close to the one true God, and He will draw close to you.*
James 4:7-8 (Voice)

(Words in parentheses added by the author for clarity.)

"Since the beginning, our loving Creator has been pursuing us, drawing us closer to Him. He invites us to move closer to Him so we can be fully His."

The above quotation is written in the Voice Translation Bible right under these verses of scripture. This is the purpose of submission; it's all about entrustment. Our Heavenly Father desires for each of us to rely on Him fully.

SUBMISSION DEFINED

Let's look at the definition of the word *submit: to give over or yield to the power or authority of another*. It means *to defer to another's opinion, decision, or judgment*. Again, this is about the One we submit our lives to, having our best interest at heart. Who better to submit to first of all than to our Father in Heaven? Before we can even begin to submit to a spouse, we must be submitted to God. Our submission puts us in the place of giving ourselves in an uncompromising relationship with the One we say we love. For how can we humbly submit ourselves, our lives in totality, without loving entirely the one we're submitting to? This submission by love is the ultimate act of surrender. This is what God requires and desires because He always has our best interest at the heart of it! Submission to God is first! I can't reiterate that enough!

Yet, there are different levels of submission. For instance, there's submission to authority in the workplace, society, and to those more knowledgeable in an area we're pursuing (Hebrews 3:17). This is submission in part because we are only under this authority temporarily. We obey traffic laws and follow the order of the different institutions. For example, when making your banking transactions, if you don't bank online, you have to stand in line listening to the directives they give you while you're in that particular establishment. That goes for the grocery store, gas station, movie theater, flying on commercial airplanes and standing in long lines at the amusement park, etc. We submit to whatever is desired and required when we're in those establishments.

We are submitted to the authorities that govern everywhere we go and for whatever period we're in a particular place. This everyday submission is required for the maintaining of an organized existence. It's vital for us to be able to flourish in this organized mechanism called our society. When there's no submission in these areas, there's chaos, as we've witnessed throughout our world.

Now, chaos can ensue because of the abuse of power by those given the authority. That's when rebellion kicks in, and governments and legislations are turned upside down or right side up, depending on who's looking. Just to put a note here, that's what the disciples of Christ were being accused of doing when they went around spreading the Gospel of Jesus Christ (Acts 17:6). But in fact, these men and women were not trying to tear things up or turn things upside down; they were completely submitted to the laws of the land as they carried out their work for Christ. I just wanted to put a pen here because it may appear that these men and women were disruptive in their tactics when they were not. They were treated harshly for their faith because the teachings of Jesus Christ threatened those in authority.

These authorities believed that what they perceived as radical teaching would overturn their government and would disrupt their way of life. In reality, the only people who were truly threatened were those who profited from the ignorance of the people who followed their unsubstantiated teachings. Those who felt threatened by the words and the ways of the disciples stirred up those in high-ranking positions to bring their campaign for Christ under question. That is really what the uproar was all about.

It reminds me of the Civil Rights movement. It was unrest against authority because those in charge abused their power. It's not that the Civil Rights movement was not a just cause; it threatened those who profited from the disenfranchisement of the minority. That was a sidebar on why 'good trouble' is sometimes needed, as coined by Civil Rights Activist John Lewis, who became a United States Congressman.

Changing systems and laws for the inclusion of all people to be treated justly and fairly is always a good thing, especially for all people who behave just and fairly. God never intended for you or me to submit to abuse and misuse or tyrannical behavior; that is not His desire for us! Why would a just God want us to be abused and misused if He loves us? He does not! That is precisely why submission is not given blindly but wisely, considering what and who we're submitting to.

People have thought that submission is something you must do without careful consideration and sometimes constant evaluation. Not to say we should heavily scrutinize every person's actions to see if they are worthy of our submission; come on now, that's not what I'm saying! You have an inner Witness that will help you submit and discern when something isn't quite right. You also have common sense, which is sometimes one and the same. Even when you may have an unruly boss, you have a choice to either submit or quit. You should weigh the cost of that decision. Or you can listen to the Word of God.

If your boss is angry at you, don't quit! A quiet spirit can overcome even great mistakes.
Ecclesiastes 10:4 (NLT)

Sometimes if we can just quiet and calm ourselves, we can get by the bluster of a boss who has anger issues by just holding our peace. The King James Version of that verse says, ***"if the spirit of the ruler rises up against you, leave not your place,"*** meaning stay in a place of submission. It goes on to say because "your yielding pacifies great offenses." Simply stated, we can humbly submit, whether right or wrong. We're not being abused, just perhaps misunderstood. If you've offended your boss, submit; if your boss has offended you, guess what, you can still submit!

Submission is a serious choice. To have someone submit to you is a heavy responsibility that should not be taken lightly. With God as their Help, that person can, for the most part, handle the caring and careful handling of someone's life, but without Him, they may not be able to do so effectively. We need the Help of God in both arenas!

SUBMISSION=SAFETY

Yet and still, as we trust in the Lord as our Leader and Guide, we can obey His Word and take Him at His Word when the scriptures encourage us, each and every one of us, to submit. Submission is the Biblical principle we must employ as believers in Christ Jesus. Submission is the starting point for every believer in Christ; it's the leverage to be the living witness for those around us to see. Our behavior is the most significant statement of our stand in Christ. What we do, not just what we say, matters.

"Submit yourselves to [the authority of] every human institution for the sake of the Lord [to honor His name], whether it is to a king as one in a position of power, or to governors as sent by him to bring punishment to those who do wrong, and to praise and encourage those who do right. For it is the will of God

that by doing right you may silence (muzzle, gag) the [culpable] ignorance and irresponsible criticisms of foolish people. Live as free people, but do not use your freedom as a cover or pretext for evil, but [use it and live] as bond-servants of God. Show respect for all people [treat them honorably], love the brotherhood [of believers], fear God, honor the king."
1 Peter 2:13-17 AMP

This is the life of submission that we should walk in every day as believers, as Leading Ladies. Honestly, if you're in the workforce or living in society, you're already operating in it. Now, with more clarity of mind, we see the optimized goal of it. This is a part of how we advance the cause of Christ. When we honor and love one another as brothers and sisters in Christ, we can also respect those in authority over us.

A new commandment I give unto you, That ye love one another; as I have loved you, that ye also love one another. By this shall all men know that ye are my disciples, if ye have love one to another.
John 13:34-35 (KJV)

This word love is the Greek word **agape**. In The New Strong's Expanded Dictionary of Bible Words, it means **affection, good will, and benevolence**. It can also mean **to give a love feast or a feast of love**. If we know anything about a feast, there's always abundance; it's filling and fun. Love is how we should treat one another, which the world should see from us.

Giving an abundance of love and respect is so fulfilling that it fills each of us up until we overflow! So much so that those who witness it will want to get in on the fun! This is how God loves us, and we should be an extension of that same love to others. This agape love is what should be given to one another especially those who are married!

I love this title from the New Living Translation.

SPIRIT-GUIDED RELATIONSHIPS: WIVES AND HUSBANDS

And further, submit to one another out of reverence for Christ. For wives, this means submit to your husbands as to the Lord. For a husband is the head of his wife as Christ is the head of the church. He is the Savior of his body, the church. As the church submits to Christ, so you wives should submit to your husbands in everything.
Ephesians 5:21-25 (NLT)

For husbands, this means love your wives, just as Christ loved the church. He gave up his life for her.

This is a beautiful depiction of the synergy of submission, which produces a beautiful effect for the advancement of the family. We see here in Ephesians the order in which submission takes place. The first thing mentioned is submitting to one another in your relationship in honor and respect to the Lord. Not just in our marital relationships but to every person we're in communion with. The Message Bible Translation says, ***"be courteously reverent to one another."*** Another way to translate this scripture is by defining it as "holding each other up in the highest esteem." It means to prefer one another over or before yourself.

Let's place a parenthetical pause here to mention that if you can be kind and courteous to everyone but your spouse, you are most definitely not aligning with the scriptures! I'm sure you've come across the saying, "Charity begins at home," and that's where loving, respecting, and honoring each other should start and flow from (1 Timothy 5:8)! When this is accomplished or continued, we have the second order of submission: wives submitting to their own husband; this is placing yourself in the care of your husband. It's a two-part word: 'sub' to come under or to place yourself under the 'mission.'

You must place yourself in the subordinate position because no one can do it but you. A rank structure needs to be in place for the mission to be carried out effectively. Not because one is better than the other; it's simply the order of placement. Sometimes, the one leading the way only sees what's directly in front of them, perhaps even what may be a long way off, but the one following can look and see everything around them. This is a military procedure in times of war on the battlefield. Believers operating in this world can understand this. This is what the military term "I've got your six" means; I've got your blind spot; you don't have to worry about looking behind you or around you because I've got you. You're looking ahead and to the sides of you, and I'm looking behind and around; we're in this together!

This place of submission is a place of safety. When we submit to God, we come under the mission of God, where we are safe and receive His full support and protection. When we are submitted to God, we're allowing Him to lead, guide and direct our lives. When a husband and wife are in the proper alignment with God first and then each other, this act of submission for the wife is a place of safety and protection as well.

She comes under, and he covers her, shields her, and protects her. It's not cowering down like an animal being beaten and abused. Submission is the supportive role in the marriage relationship and sometimes the most important role in the relationship. A husband needs his wife's support, it adds fuel to his life and fire to his soul, and it fills him up so he can keep going forward. As he covers you, you care for him; in turn, as he cares for you, you cover him.

The third is the husband's responsibility to be Christ-like in his actions towards his wife. He first loves his wife like Christ loves the church and gives up his life for his wife as Christ gave up His life for the church. This may seem like a hard saying to give up one's life in totality for someone else. However, Christ laid down His life because of His deep love for the church. He laid down His life because He desired an intimate relationship with the church. So, how can we as believers in Christ not give our lives completely to the One Who laid down His life for us? In the same way, a covenant is made in marriage, which is a contract to keep, cover, and protect the wife with whom God has entrusted to the husband.

Jesus Christ is our example in this holy arrangement.

Submission is a gift given to the one who receives it. It's precious and should not be handled harshly (Colossians 3:19). To give up one's life to another in the act of commitment and love is a major sacrifice that should be received with reverence and awe. This is the divine purpose of Christ concerning the covenant of marriage. This is the purpose of the act of submission in all areas of our walk in Christ.

We understand we're not perfect, but we're always striving towards our godly goals. Don't stop desiring to be better and to do better. Our God is present in every situation throughout every season to help us along the way. All six of these characteristics are blueprints for the everyday God-inspired Leading Lady.

The Leading Lady Sees
The Leading Lady Speaks
The Leading Lady Stands
The Leading Lady Surrenders
The Leading Lady Sacrifices
The Leading Lady Submits

CHAPTER 8

Jump Lady!

"Do one thing every day that scares you."
ELEANOR ROOSEVELT

A friend of mine just brought the following traumatic experience back to my remembrance the other day. She knows who she is, so I won't mention her name! Ok, it wasn't that traumatizing, but I was still scared, nonetheless! Years ago, my husband and I went on vacation with a couple of pastor friends to Mexico. My beloved spouse loves to do excursions when we travel to different places.

Excursions are fun activities that people enjoy when taking trips to foreign lands or maybe not so foreign, but just to different places. This particular adventure took place in the water, the Pacific Ocean, to be exact. The fish swam right up next to us and around us as we rode by! The experience was on an underwater bike that traveled just a short distance all around on the ocean floor, allowing us to look up close and personal at the different types of midsize marine life that inhabit the area.

A large boat takes the mighty adventurers out to a spot in the middle of the ocean to partake in the fun! You get on this bike, placing your head under a large glass dome that looks like a huge upside-down fishbowl. Although your entire body is submerged underwater, your head is completely encapsulated with nothing but breathable air! This air is filtered through a tube to each underwater motorbike. It was quite a pretty cool thing! I know this reads like an exciting exploration, doesn't it?! Perhaps to you, it seems absolutely crazy; either way, we did it!

This wasn't our first underwater experience of this kind; this was our second of many! Because our friends had never done anything remotely like this before, we decided to allow them all to go ahead of us. As you probably can understand, these things can be a bit scary, especially to the non-swimmers in the group; even the swimmers were leary of this contraption. So, it took some time getting everyone situated. Due to unforeseen circumstances, not everyone was able to partake in this underwater journey.

Well, I'd like to point out here that I am a non-swimmer even though I participate in many different water activities. I do it because I want to face my fears. I especially do it because my husband is always with me, and he is a good swimmer. So, I have a smidgeon of peace, knowing he's with me and will risk life and limb to save me if the occasion should arise!

Well, this time, although he jumped right in the water and

got his head under the glass dome, his ears began to pop and ring as they attempted to lower him down to the ocean floor. It was about 20 or so feet down to the bottom. The trick, if you would, is to equalize your system by blowing in your mouth while keeping it closed to pop your ears. The feeling is equal to traveling up or down a high mountain, an elevator, or going on a plane. Your ears pop. Due to a bit of irregularity in his ears, he couldn't equalize enough to stay underwater without extreme pain, so he came back up and waited on the surface of the ocean.

THE DESCENT

Now, I'm the last to get on the motorized bike after most of our beautiful friends were safely down under the deep water. The tour guides are now in a hurry because there's only so much oxygen for each underwater motorbike. Because so much time was used trying to get everyone situated and semi-comfortable, we needed to get moving. For those who don't swim, the guides were supposed to bring the bike up to the water's surface right next to the boat. Then this would allow me or another non-swimmer to sit securely on the bike as I gently place my head under the glass dome, lowering me slowly down to the bottom deep so that we can begin our underwater travel with the fish.

Yep, you guessed it. That did not happen. As I waited on the side of the boat for my bike, the tour guide in the middle of the ocean yelled loudly with his powerful accent, "Just jump in; we need to get going!" I proceeded to yell back, "But I can't swim!" The bike was way too far out in the water for my comfort. So, I waited in the boat for them to bring it to me so that I could get on as comfortably as possible! That is what was supposed to happen! That is how they instructed us it would be done; this is what I expected! That is what I wanted!

Instead, he yells back at me, "Jump Lady and swim to me." I shout back louder, "I! Can't! Swim!" I'm looking at my husband, who's in the middle of the water watching, and he encourages me to go ahead and jump in as the tour guide yells again even louder at me, "Jump Lady! Jump Lady! Jump!!! Lady!!!" So, I took a deep breath, looked right into the deep ocean, closed my eyes, then I went ahead and **jumped**!

*"What would life be if we had
no courage to attempt anything?"*
VINCENT VAN GOGH

*"Each of us must confront our own fears,
must come face to face with them.
How we handle our fears will determine
where we go with the rest of our lives.
To experience adventure or
to be limited by the fear of it."*
JUDY BLUME

FEAR CAN BE A PRETTY COMPLEX THING

A healthy fear that causes your antennas to come up due to an unforeseen danger is essential! This type of fear gives off warning signals that cause you to be more alert, aware, and acute to your surroundings or circumstances. It keeps you from doing things like walking down dark alleys at night alone, driving recklessly up and down winding roads on the side of mountain cliffs, or walking into certain places or situations that our senses tell us may be harmful! You get the idea. At least, I hope this is what healthy fear does for you!

On the other hand, fear can cause you to be paralyzed into inaction. This is the type of fear that needs to be worked through and ultimately conquered. Fear of failure, fear of success, fear of the future, fear of the unknown, and many other fears similar to these are genuine fears. However, these types of fears can be debilitating in their consumption of our psyche. Leaving you stuck with no forward motivation to draw you closer to your purpose in fulfilling your destined future! Yet in this gift called life, we must make the case to face our fears, and the best way to face these fears is to meet them with faith in our God!

What time I am afraid, I will trust in thee. In God I will praise his word, in God I have put my trust; I will not fear what flesh can do unto me.
Psalms 56:3-4 (KJV)

THE SUM OF ALL FEARS

I'm sure you've come to the understanding that I don't swim, which stems from a fear of water coming from my childhood by not being appropriately introduced to the aspect of swimming. Meaning, my mom scared me to pieces about swimming, and it stuck with me. It's not really that I can't swim, it's more like I don't swim, or I won't swim. I haven't built enough confidence in my swimming skills to partake in the exercise without feelings of apprehension. Wearing a life vest at all times and having my husband by my side while participating in water activities helps me conquer my fear of water, which is a fear of drowning and ultimately the fear of death by water!

Apostle Holcomb called this fear of death the *Sum of All Fears*. It's the ultimate fear that is the precursor for a lot of the other fears. I know this is very morbid right? But this might just be a real fear that each one of us may need to be willing to face. If not in this particular case, perhaps we've built up a complex or fear in some other area.

So, when I become afraid to participate in water activities, I begin to place my trust in the Lord. First, I talk to Him about my fear, and then He gives me His Peace. Next, I calm my breathing, which calms my anxiety, and then I jump full force into that scary thing called water. Sometimes, those conversations with the Lord are a bit longer than others, depending on the depth of the situation or the body of water.

ADVENTURES OVER FEAR

Because I understand the process of getting over my fear of water, I intentionally participate in adventures to conquer it. That has included Sea-Doos, jet skis, and driving or riding on small boats across lakes and ocean depths. Snorkeling and underwater bicycling, which I've shared, are also part of the list. Repelling down 250-foot drops along waterfalls several times and climbing up a huge waterfall can be added to the adventures. I have also participated in parasailing over the ocean. It's beautiful up there, by the way, and so peaceful hanging out in the sky. Bungee swinging into lakes, white water rafting, and sliding down a waterslide from hundreds of feet high off the side of a mountain, only once, has been added to the chronicles. Even going down a lazy river on an inner tube can frighten me.

Let me just say that we make sure everything we do is safe and has the proper equipment and tools to handle the adventure we are partaking in. If we're in a group setting, there's always more than one good swimmer. Notice, I said we; I never do these things alone! And yet, with all of this, I'm always scared the first time. It gets much better the second and third time, and it's always fun, every time! Please note that fear can be a detriment to your future faith walk with the Father.

> *"I have learned over the years*
> *that when one's mind is made up,*
> *this diminishes fear; knowing what must be done*
> *does away with fear."*
> ROSA PARKS

BUNGEE JUMP IN FAITH

This life of faith that we live with the Father is only fulfilled and becomes fulfilling when we take those leaps of faith with Him. Ok, it may not always necessarily be leaps of faith with the Lord; it should be a walk of faith with Him. I say with Him because we have no guarantee that we won't fail without Him. Even when we do stumble, He's right there picking us up, every time and anytime we need Him. God is perfect that way.

I'm entirely aware of the premise of falling forward and

tripping up. I think if you're going to trip, up is the best way to go! Sometimes, the mess-ups and the trip-ups are the learning experiences to help us go up and grow up. So, we must make sure to always get up from the fall or the failed attempt. Building up our courage and strength with every experience we encounter is like an apparatus placed around us that will help us jump safely. When you pick yourself up and try again, you build more skills for the next go around!

For instance, if you've ever done a bungee jump once, you have the confidence to do it again. Because you trust the equipment the bungee cord and the harness wrapped around you has you secure, you know you will never hit the ground. The equipment used, the apparatus secured around you, holds you in place for the jump. So, you can let go and jump freely, flying down through the air for those few moments and then bouncing back because you're secure, locked in tight with the bungee cord and harness.

Therefore, this is why you can always jump without gripping or having paralyzing fear. So, when you've made a step and stumbled, Jesus picks you up. When you've made a leap and tumbled, Jesus lifts you up. When you've made a jump, and it seemed like everything crumbled, Jesus is right there putting you and everything else back together again. So really, Jesus is your apparatus! He has you so secure in the Harness of His Hold that when you jump out to where He's calling out for you to be, you can do it without fear of failing and never recovering. *You build confidence by facing your fears.*

Dr. Halene Giddens

THE LOVE TRIANGLE

This walk with God gives you the ability to succeed in ways you'd never imagine! Making every step you take a step of faith with your God should be your desired goal. Challenging yourself in the area of faith is so worth the jump, the leap, and every step you make.

Having your Heavenly Father as the center and the circumference of your life is supposed to be *satisfying*, *securing*, and even *stimulating*. The first part of the love triangle is that He satisfies. Why? Because when coming to know God and Who He is along with Who He desires to be in your life, which by the way is everything, you become totally fulfilled.

Falling in love with Jesus is one of the most incredible journeys you can take! This is one of the best ways to get to know God with an open heart of love and acceptance. Receiving His Love for you and then loving Him in return should always be growing and developing because the more you know of Him, the more of Himself He reveals to you!

It's like looking through a kaleidoscope of colors ever-changing, always illuminating—a prism of all kinds of different dimensions of color and design. That's what our God is like—a million different beautiful, bright qualities, reflections. It's an extraordinary experience coming to know Him more and more! There's nothing like it on this planet!

169

But as for me, my hope is to see Your face.
When I am vindicated, I will look upon the holy face of
God, and when I awake, the longing of my soul will be
satisfied in the glow of Your presence.
Psalms 17:15 (The Voice)

"I will fill the soul of the priests with abundance,
And My people will be satisfied with My goodness,"
declares the LORD.
Jeremiah 31:14 (NASB)

(Underlined words are added by the author for emphasis.)

Oh, there's so much satisfaction in God! He's right there with you every step of the way, especially in those times when you begin to face your fears! He wants to be with you for all of it, not just the big moments, the challenging moments, the moments of despair and disappointments, but all of the moments of your life: the big, the small, and every single moment in between. God wants you to live satisfied in Him. The void that may be festering in your heart can only be satisfied by Him (Col. 2:10; Eph. 3:19).

SECURITY!

Then, there's the security found in trusting Him. The Word of God in *Psalm 56:3* says, *"What time,"* which means anytime, *"I am afraid I will trust in You."* There are so many scriptures about trusting God; the main thing He's trying to get us to do is to trust in Him.

That is really what the guide in our ocean experience was trying to get me to do! No, actually, he was just trying to get me in the water, on that underwater bike, so he could get that tour started and to get me to trust him. My husband was trying to get me to trust him by saying, "Although you think you can't swim, you can be assured that all will be well." And it was! Oh, how comforting to know that Someone always has you, right in the middle of the deep! Let me remind you that there is Someone that constantly has you, and He always will!

That dude, the tour guide, I mean, took me by the neck, shoved me on that bike so fast, and then placed my head right in that big upside-down fish bowl filled with breathable air! At least, I think that's what happened after I jumped; it all took place so quickly! I was indignant at first until I realized I was completely fine as I was slowly lowered down to the ocean floor so that our adventure could begin. Then, because I decided to trust, my fear was abated; that's the reason I went ahead and jumped to begin enjoying my journey.

Sometimes, trusting God when fear hits your heart can be just like that. One moment fear is gripping your heart, making it pound uncontrollably! Then you go through the things that have you fearful because you're trusting God. You say to yourself, "Hey, that really wasn't so bad," or "It was completely awful," but you made it to the other side unscathed! You are probably the better for it!

That's when you become secure in knowing your God is with you in it all! He's got you, He's holding you, He's helping you, you're making it! Another triumph of faith!

*"The Lord is for me, so I will have no fear.
What can mere people do to me?*
Psalms 118:6 NLT

Every time you have an adventure in faith conquering your fear, you get another notch of security in trusting your God! You become confident in the God Who holds your purpose in His Hand! You're getting closer to accomplishing all that God has for you on this side of life!

Then you would trust, because there is hope; And you would look around and rest securely.
Job 11:18 (NASB)
(Underlined words are added by the author for emphasis.)

LOVE STIMULATES

Stimulating is the adventure and the excitement connected to living for God and letting Him lead the way in your life. God desires to challenge us to do more, go further, reach higher and obtain greater! God is not satisfied with where you are currently, and neither should you be! It's not even about making gigantic life-altering decisions; it's about each and every day allowing God to lead you every step of the way. Perhaps sometimes making those huge faith-based jumps.

I love this definition for the word *stimulating: to rouse to action or effort by encouragement or pressure; to spur on and incite, excite, and invigorate.* Oh, my goodness, does this not describe how the Lord moves us forward into action towards our destined purpose?! God's hope for you is to be roused into motivated, stimulated purpose, and that's exciting!

Instead of being fearful of the unknown, look forward to your future with the eyes of faith! Get excited about what God has for you, anticipating not that your future is frightening and scary, but that what the Lord has for you personally, Leading Lady, is exciting, even intriguing!

I hope you're ready to jump! Your Heavenly Father is right out there in the deep, ready to take you by the neck, I mean the hand, and lead you into the deep waters of your faith-filled future!

Deep calls to deep in the roar of your waterfalls; all your breakers and your billows have swept over me. The Lord will send his faithful love by day; his song will be with me in the night — a prayer to the God of my life.
Psalms 42:7-8 CSB

THE DEEP IS CALLING YOU

God is calling us out there where He is, and sometimes He's right out there in the deep. Are you ready to jump? Here's an excellent way to look at your faith-filled **JUMP:**

JUMP
Jesus
Undergirding
My
Purpose

When it's the Lord leading your jump into the deep, He's the One Who's upholding you the whole time. He's the One Who will make sure the waters don't overflow or overwhelm you. Walking or jumping into why you're here on earth takes allowing God to calm the anxiety of your heart—allowing Him to maneuver you right to the edge of the bank so that you can see the possibilities of what you can do!

When you allow your thoughts, desires, and actions to be managed by Him, He will direct you to the *satisfied*, *secured*, and *stimulated* life you were created to have.

VOCATION VS. OCCUPATION: WHAT'S YOUR MOTIVATION FOR THE JUMP?

As a prisoner of the Lord, I urge you:
Live a life that is worthy of the calling He has
graciously extended to you. Be humble. Be gentle.
Be patient. Tolerate one another in an atmosphere
thick with love. Make every effort to preserve
the unity the Spirit has already created,
with peace binding you together.
Ephesians 4:1-3 (Voice)

In this particular scripture, the Apostle Paul is speaking to the people who lived in Ephesus. He was in prison in Rome during this written letter, but because of his calling, he couldn't help but continue to write and encourage people all over the world as he knew it at that time. Ephesians 4:3 in the King James Version uses the word vocation for the word calling. Paul writes to the believers to walk worthy of the vocation of which you've been called. How does he suggest we do this: by being humble, gentle, patient, and tolerant of others, loving people unconditionally. The calling by God's Love for you requires being motivated to walk in your vocation, and it should be employed to fulfill your occupation. The fulfillment of both vocation and occupation will be fulfilling when you keep humility, gentleness, patience, and love as your motivator.

When it comes to jumping into the things you desire to do, the things that have been deep down on the inside of you, you've got to be aware of the area on the spectrum you're to operate from. Sometimes, your vocation is your occupation, and other times your vocation is funded by your occupation. Your vocation is that in which God has called you to do. It is your divine call covered by God's Grace to accomplish the desired goal, and this is not just centered on religious acts or services, although it can be.

Your vocation may even occasionally take much labor, but it's a labor of love, and everyone around you experiences this beautiful special ability that you bring to life. It pulls you; it drives you; it keeps you pumped! Sometimes, it's what you dream about and what stirs the motors in your mind because of the creative ideas that come to you concerning it! It's what you really enjoy doing. It can bring others joy and fulfillment around you, and you're pretty good at it!

Here's a great definition of vocation found in Wikipedia: *A vocation (from Latin vocatio 'a call, summons') is an occupation to which a person is especially drawn or for which they are suited, trained, or qualified. Though now often used in non-religious contexts, the meanings of the term originated in Christianity.*

Your occupation is usually your primary source of income, which generally stems from your work or business; it's how you pay your bills, meaning the way you earn a living. It's your livelihood, how you make it in this world of commerce. Sometimes, people love what they get paid to do, and others have occupations they don't care for. It's always great to love what pays your bills or at least like it a little bit. Perhaps at best, tolerate what you do until what you would rather be doing comes along, or you make the preparations to be able to go after the thing you love to do, and it pays you!

These two things, your vocation and occupation, can collide. Another way of saying it is, they can fold into each other, or one can also be an extension of the other, and that's pretty great! Meaning, the thing you love to do provides for the things you love to do, and then, sometimes, the thing you get paid to do is the very thing you love to do!

You must acknowledge the difference and where you are in the journey. Then, when these areas are distinctively defined, you have a better understanding of what you may be jumping into or more to the point of what it may cost you to make the jump! Which may indeed be everything, but so worth the price!

Your Heavenly Father has His Hand on all types of gifts, skills, and purposes, all of which are necessary from the tiniest of inclinations to what we'd like to look at as significant career choices, so nothing is wasted in the Hands of the Father.

In actuality, when God is leading you towards your vocation, He is funding the bill either through you or for you. You've got to *discern the difference*, which is to *perceive, recognize, see*, not by just your intellect, but by the Spirit of the Lord Who's always with you and Who lives in you! You may not always have a clear picture of what's out there in the deep, but at least you can know when God is calling you out there and how long you need to stay and what price you need to pay.

Although sometimes along the way, God shifts you and changes you and broadens and brightens the path (Psalms 16:11, 119:35; Proverbs 4:18). He doesn't change, but He does change you, always guiding you and even preparing you for what's next (Malachi 3:16). That has to be the Harness for your jump: the Spirit of the Lord leading you out there in the deep!

One thing is for sure, He is leading you forward, He is calling you upward, and He just may be beckoning you to jump. So, go ahead and Jump Lady!

"Work Hard! Stay Humble!
Be Kind! Take the Leap!"
DAVID ANDREW KRUPSKI

Igniting The Leading Lady In You

CHAPTER 9

It's Not Over, Keep Going

"Everything is Temporary,
Including bad moments. KEEP GOING."
CHARLOTTE BAILEY

L ittle Foot, the dinosaur in the epic, animated motion picture *The Land Before Time*, yelled out when his world was changing and crumbling around him to his little dinosaur friends, trailing behind him, and I quote, ***"We've got to keep going!"*** Their existence, as they knew, was changing. The place where Little Foot and his family lived had become uninhabitable. There had been word of another place, a better place, for them to live, thrive and grow; all species of dinosaurs were trying to get to that special place they had heard about.

In the journey, Little Foot becomes separated from his grandparents; his parents died early on. But Little Foot, although alone and scared, kept moving forward on his journey because he knew he couldn't just stop where he was and give up. He had to make every effort to get to that new land, that better place he'd heard all about. On his way, he met other little dinosaurs, who were also alone and afraid and didn't know what to do or which way to go.

And so, because there's always strength in numbers, the band of little dinosaurs went through hardships and trials, conquering their greatest fears (one of which was being eaten by a Tyrannosaurus Rex! I mean, who wouldn't be afraid of that!). They even had to go through their own inner turmoil of doubt, fear, and unbelief (I know, pretty deep for an animated movie), but they made it together to the Great Valley.

"No matter how much we try to avoid negative events, they always seem to find us. When something bad happens we often have the tendency to soak in our own misery and think we don't have what it takes to keep going.... The truth is things never get easier, we just find better ways in overcoming obstacles and learn to not dwell on them as much. So the key to keep going is in our pockets."
FLAVIA MEDRUT

"Believe in yourself, take on your challenges, dig deep within yourself to conquer fears. Never let anyone bring you down. You gotta keep going."
CHANTAL SUTHERLAND

AGE IS NOT A DETERRENT FROM YOUR DIVINE ASSIGNMENT

In the book of Joshua, this man of God had the assignment to take over where the servant of the Lord, Moses, left off. Joshua was to bring the children of Israel into the Promised Land. This was the place the Lord had for them to inhabit and possess as their very own. Mind you, this was millions of people Joshua had to contend with, definitely a huge undertaking for him (Joshua 1:1)! They were to go from 400 years as slaves to prosperous landowners!

Joshua remained faithful to the Lord, leading the armies of the Living God in every battle, conquering their enemies from coast to coast. Whichever direction the Lord led Joshua is the way he'd take the children of Israel with boldness and courage just as God had instructed him to do (Joshua 1:1-9). These folks were tearing things up and taking names as they went! God was like, "It's not time to take sides! It's time to take over! Keep it moving and possess the land!" In some war assignments the Lord led them into, they didn't even have to fight! They just had to obey the instructions of the Lord!

Now, there was one battle in a small city called Ai. Joshua and the elders of the Israeli families decided to send only a couple thousand men out to fight. Just a small number of troops, nothing significant. Israel's army lost that particular battle with the men running and fleeing for their lives from their enemy. This was all because of one selfish act by a man named Achan, who kept some of the goods he found from the previous battle and hid the items amongst his stuff. The only problem with this was the children of Israel had promised to give everything they received from that particular battle in Jericho to the Lord. So, they decided not to take anything for themselves but allow all the riches they collected to be kept in the treasury of the Lord (Joshua 6:19).

Joshua then sought the Lord to find out what in the world went wrong! As soon as Joshua and the children of Israel understood what happened, they dealt severely with the deliberate disobedience of Achan, who caused trouble to come upon the entire camp of Israel. God's Hand of Deliverance was with them once again to conquer their enemies! They were able to keep all of the spoils and the loot they retrieved from that next battle because the Lord told Joshua they could have it (Joshua 8:27)! Their total obedience was the key to their complete victory! Every time Joshua followed the instructions and leadings of the Lord, Israel always prevailed! When Joshua didn't consult the Lord, things got a little sticky. But praise God, Joshua always knew how to backtrack and get it right!

After many years of him doing the Lord's bidding to benefit God's beloved people and obtaining acres of land for the children of Israel to dwell in and raise their families, the Lord spoke to Joshua.

Now Joshua was old and stricken in years;
and the LORD said unto him,
Thou art old and stricken in years,
and there remaineth yet very much land to be possessed.
Joshua 13:1 (KJV)

Basically, God was saying to Joshua it's not over; the work is not finished! You may have gotten older, yet there's still a purpose for your existence in your latter years. You haven't completed your assignment yet, so you have to **keep going**!

And that's the word for each one of us Leading Ladies: there's still much to accomplish; there's still much land to possess. Although we may have to pause and take a break or even backtrack and start over, we are always supposed to keep going. There is still more in store. We still have places to go, things to see, and things to do when we get there. As long as there's breath in our lungs and strength in our physical bodies, we are capable of going, doing, and seeing more. Even if you don't have strength in your body, you have strength in your mind! If you didn't, you wouldn't be able to read and comprehend this book right now. This is not about how old you are or how many years or how much time you have left on this side of life! There is still so much more you have to offer, and every little thing you do and every little step you take does count for something!

They will be like trees that stay healthy and fruitful,
even when they are old. And they will say about you,
"The Lord always does right! God is our mighty rock.
Psalms 92:14-15 (CEV)

Your contribution is still needed; it's why you're still here! You're still living and breathing for a reason, and it's not just to live and breathe. You've got thoughts; you have emotions; you have purpose, so stir up your passion! You have a voice! How do I know? If you've got lungs full of air, a sound box in your body, and you can formulate a sentence, you have a voice, and someone is listening! What are you saying?! *The Leading Lady Speaks*, so choose your words wisely; they're important!

There may be those behind you or looking up to you who may need you to give a helping hand occasionally and pull them to their next place. Then there are those you need to aspire to in front of you, who can push you to your next step. Either way, there's always something more you can do! It's in you to keep going! Hopefully, I'm speaking health, hope, life, and strength into you, even in this written format. You're being infused with the wherewithal to complete your next chapter in this life's story! As Martin would continually say to Gina, "Get to steppin'!" What I mean by this is the good kind of steppin'! The steppin' that causes you to always keep going. The steps it takes for you to get to that next platform, turn the next page, and get to that next stage! Steppin' forward and, yes, sometimes steppin' out of the front door! Steppin' into your best. Steppin' into what's next! Steppin' into success!

The steps of a good man (and woman) are ordered
by the LORD, And He delights in his (and her) way.
Though he (and she) fall, he (and she)
shall not be utterly cast down; For the LORD
upholds him (and her) with His hand.
Psalms 37:23-24 (NKJV)

(Words in parentheses added by the author for emphasis.)

Leading Lady, the steps that you take with your God are

orchestrated, directed, and established by the Lord. He wants you to take the steps; He desires for you to keep going, keep living, keep giving, and keep growing. He's already laid the path; all you need to do is step into it. This takes getting to know Him through His Word and prayer so that you can go with Him and grow with Him! I've already stated this prior to this chapter, so let's recognize that it's important to enjoy fellowship with our God. The steps you take are a part of your growth process. You have to be willing to let the Lord lead you in the path that's just for you! The path that's right for you is the steps He's ordered for you; they are the perfect steps... just for you!

If you're feeling stagnant, just get up, shake yourself, and take the steps. Don't stop where you are right now and say you have arrived. Instead, always say, "I'm on my way to the next place. I'm on my way to the next big thing!" That will be whatever is big, better, or best for you!

CLIMBING WATERFALLS

"As long as you keep going, you'll keep getting better. And as you get better, you gain more confidence. That alone is success."
TAMARA TAYLOR

About 10 years ago, after my first back surgery, my husband and I went on vacation with another couple to Jamaica. As it rained the majority of our stay, we had a good time anyway. One of the adventures we partook of during our visit was to climb up a waterfall called Dunn's Rivers Falls. It's one of the major natural attractions most visitors and locals look forward to enjoying.

It had been a nice sunny day when we started out early that morning. We had gone through a garden tour with beautiful Jamaican flowers and shrubbery. We were taking pictures and enjoying the scenery. We walked to the area where the falls were located, and after listening to all the instructions from our tour guides, we were ready to begin our climb. Unfortunately, as soon as we took our first step at the bottom of the waterfall, it began to pour down rain! Whelp, since we were already there in place and ready to go and we paid our money, we began our journey upward to the top of the Falls.

One of the instructions from our tour guides was for us to make sure we took care of the person in front of us and behind us being aware that they were safe on the rocks as we all climbed up the falls. Since it was raining, the rocks were a bit more slippery than usual. It was a waterfall, so of course, the water was gushing down over the rocks along with the pelting rainfall that came down on our heads from above. It was an adventure indeed!

As we began our ascent up the steep cliffs of the falls, I realized my legs had very little strength to climb. We didn't consider that after my surgery, and because I hadn't done much walking, let alone exercise, my legs would be weak. Therefore, I needed some help. As instructed by the guides, each person assisted someone around them, ensuring that they climbed up the falls the right and safe way. Everyone needed to climb safely, or it could've been a detriment to the others who followed behind. It was a community climb for sure!

With our friends ahead of me and my husband behind me, I was helped up each rock and assisted up every climb from behind. It was more like I was pulled up each rock and pushed up from behind, literally, just to clarify. Either way, I made the climb! There would have been no possible way for me to make that climb on my own without all their help. Not only was I able to climb to the top of the falls, but I even jumped in a few of the ponds along the way! Honestly, that wasn't my choice; it was a part of the adventure. So once again, I jumped.

My friend said we laughed and cried the entire way up, but it was hard to tell with the rain coming down upon our heads relentlessly. However, as soon as our feet hit the top of the falls, the rain immediately stopped! Can you believe that? Our entire hike up the mountain, rain poured down consistently with no break! Then the sun came out, and we went from soaking wet to being dried off from the heat of the sun! That was really something! The view from the top of the Falls was absolutely beautiful! Even the view at the bottom while looking up was pretty amazing! We enjoyed the entire experience. It was incredible, it was awesome, it was scary, and it was fun! What a journey! What an adventure!

It reminds me of the old adage that says, "There's always light at the end of the tunnel." It's why we should always keep going and never stop in the middle of the dark. That reminds me of another old adage, "It's always darkest before the dawn." We should always keep the mindset that although part of the journey may not be easy or it's just downright hard, we will make it up, make it over, make it out, and make it through! Always looking towards the light; always looking forward to the dawn of the new day!

During our waterfall adventure climb, a few people, not a part of our group, thought they could handle the falls without the guides and their instructions. Those few folks kept needing to be rescued from almost falling and hurting themselves severely. It was a little nerve-wracking watching them slip and slide across the large stones. The guides, of course, knew the best way to handle climbing on the rocks and the safest paths to take up the waterfall. Those of us on the tour listened and paid attention which yielded a successful experience.

It was interesting watching those who weren't in our group try to pass us climbing up the steeper, harsher rocks without assistance as the water gushed down from the falls and the rain fell from the heavens. I wanted to see if they were going to make it up faster than all of us following the tour guide's instructions. I thought they must have some type of climbing skill set the rest of us on tour didn't have. But alas, they did not. They just didn't want to wait patiently for the guides to aid them in their climb. Gratefully, no one was hurt from their attempts. Instead, the guides assisted them, telling them which rocks to step up and climb on to get them to the top of the Falls.

YOU CAN'T GO IT ALONE

In our journey called life, we're going to have some hills, valleys, flatlands, and maybe even some mud holes and some ponds to jump in just for the fun of it. In this life, there are going to be several people around you: those who'll help you up, those whom you'll help up, and those who'll act like they don't need any help and try to pass you up. There may even be those who may try to get in the way of you going up. Don't concern yourself with them; they can't hinder your way up. There may even be those who try to cause hurt or harm on your way up. Let it only help be the catalyst for you as you keep going up. Then there will be those who walk alongside you for a little while or a lifetime, enjoying the journey with you through life's ups and life's downs.

As my husband and a few of his friends often say, "Some people are with you for certain seasons and others for different reasons. There may even be those who might in some way be out for treason!" Your goal is to know who's who, know the difference, recognize them for who they are, and receive them or not for just what they are, nothing more and nothing less. Never place on a person more than what they are meant or even less than what they are supposed to be in your life. It would be good to take the time to recognize the potential, or the lack thereof, in the relationships you cultivate. Understanding it's ok in whichever role or capacity those certain ones play in your life's journey, believe that somehow you'll all make it to the top, one steady step at a time.

It's safe to say that as we walk, run, climb, and sometimes leap and jump our way through life's ups and downs, we're going to need some help along the way, and that's ok. It's the way it's meant to be. Sometimes we're going to need some assistance, and most times, we may need quite a bit of anything we can get! We really are better together; we weren't meant to be on this path alone. So, don't shun the help when it's presented to you, especially when it's given in good faith. Pride is thinking you're supposed to succeed on your own by yourself. That's not the case at all.

It's as if some people you encounter may think like Frank Sinatra used to sing, "I did it my way." If we know anything, that can't be precisely true; he may have done a few things his way, but you better believe he had some help along the way. You can't do everything by yourself, nor can you do it your own way, especially with others alongside you and around you. So, just like on all those televised awards shows—the Tonys, the Oscars, the Grammys, and the Emmys—there ought to be a list of people you should be able to stand up and thank, the ones who helped you along the way. To be grateful and thankful adds to your life more reasons to be grateful and thankful!

The directors, the writers, the engineers, the camera crew, and the stagehands should all be applauded and thanked. The lighting and sound technicians, the hair and makeup specialist along with the wardrobe personnel, the muffin man, and the water boy should all be thanked for all the accolades and applause you've received for your spectacular stage performance and your phenomenal, successful career! What? Excuse me? Oh, you say you didn't have all of that working for you! Well, who did you have? What help did you receive? What one person said, "You know what? I think you can do this!" What single individual gave you a little hand up or a small pat on the back? Even a small nudge or a suggestion that said, "I think you should try this one thing," or "Take these couple of classes," or "Here, why don't you check out this great book?" Like the book you're reading right at this very moment! (I'm smiling to myself.) What person or group of people did you look up to and aspire to be like in some way or another?

At every point in the right direction, at every slight turn you've been given to make a midterm correction, can be found a person to be thankful for in your life. Every person you look at and think, "Maybe I can do something like what they're doing," is a person you can thank. What one person helped teach and instruct you through the hard life experiences, even if they were the very ones who gave you the hard life experiences? You can look back and be thankful and grateful you've made it!

Being appreciative of those special people who have been a help, a push, or a hand up in your life is important. It may be the slightest action, the smallest unction, or it could be a million little things; it all adds up. It's all thank-worthy. You should be grateful for every little thing as well as the big things. And we should take the time to do so. As we've seen in tabloids and other news outlets, the life of professional performers is not easy; even with all the added puff and fluff, the struggles have been very real. Yet, they still stand up and are thankful and grateful for the help they've received that got them to the place where they are. And we can and should be thankful as well.

Let the peace of Christ [the inner calm of one who walks daily with Him] be the controlling factor in your hearts [deciding and settling questions that arise]. To this peace indeed you were called as members in one body [of believers]. And be thankful [to God always].
Colossians 3:15 AMP

Perhaps sometimes it may feel like, or it may seem like you're by yourself, but that's when you have to trust that you're not alone at all. There's always Someone Whose with you at all times! Just like the poem Footprints in the Sand, you see two sets of footprints in the sand while you're walking through life. However, during the hard times, you see only one set of footprints; you're not walking alone; the Lord is carrying you through your most difficult moments. So, the one set of footprints you see are not yours at all; instead, they are the Lord's. The God Who created you for success is walking beside you or carrying you through to the very end.

Hopefully, on your way, you'll take the time to look up and see the amazing view. If what you see directly in front of you doesn't look that great, lift your gaze a little higher and focus a little longer; you might be amazed. Our Heavenly Father wants to show you some things as you take this journey with Him, so pay attention to the view.

As I stated previously, as you're going along, there will be people in front of you, alongside you and maybe even coming up behind you that you will either say to yourself, "I have what it takes to aid and assist this one and that one," or "If they can do this thing or that, I can do it, too!" And, yes, you can! As I keep stating emphatically, you can do what God has put in you to do! The Word of God tells us to be followers of those who through faith and patience inherit the promises (Hebrews 6:12 KJV).

So don't allow your hearts to grow dull or lose your enthusiasm, but follow the example of those who fully

*received what God has promised because of their strong
faith and patient endurance.*
Hebrews 6:12 TPT

You can step right into their footsteps and follow the path
they've carved out until you start your own God-created,
carved-out path. There should always be someone you can look
up to. They may not be doing it exactly like you or even doing
exactly what you're doing, but there's always at least one, and
I'm sure quite a few more you can emulate! If there's a promise
in God's Word to receive, follow those who have received what
God had for them through strong faith and patient endurance.
Then receive what your Heavenly Father has for you by your
strong faith in your God (Acts 26:3; Hebrews 11:1).

---

*Such a large crowd of witnesses is all around us! So
we must get rid of everything that slows us down,
especially the sin that just won't let go. And we must
be determined to run the race that is ahead of us. We
must keep our eyes on Jesus, who leads us and makes
our faith complete. He endured the shame of being
nailed to a cross because he knew that later on he would
be glad he did. Now he is seated at the right side of
God's throne! So keep your mind on Jesus, who put up
with many insults from sinners. Then you won't get
discouraged and give up.*
Hebrews 12:1-3 (CEV)

Although the terrain of our ongoing lives may seem difficult at times, like Little Foot called out to his friends, "We have to keep going!" As we see, the Word of God shows us that some have gone before us that have witnessed the completed victory race that is also set before each one of us. We can't allow our issues, past or present circumstances, to slow us down or hold us back from running this race to the finish.

My only aim is to finish the race and complete the task the Lord Jesus has given me —the task of testifying to the good news of God's grace.
Acts 20:24 (NIV)

Let me flip the script a little bit and place this thought in your mind as well. Although we may think we've reached the pinnacle of our success, the journey doesn't have to end. You may think, just like Joshua, you've accomplished everything you needed to do, yet and still, constant forward motion is necessary for you! To keep moving is necessary; to keep thinking is important for your life. Physical movement and spiritual and natural growth are vital for a healthy quality of life. So you gotta keep that body and that mind moving!

Life keeps going. It's your choice to move on and take a chance on the unknown or stay behind, locked in your present, which will soon become your past, thinking of what could have been. Don't look back and say, "What if," instead, look forward and say those same two little words, "What if!" One is said with regret and disappointment, the other is said with anticipation and excitement! One is said with sadness and sorrow; the other is said with hope for tomorrow. So never look back unless it's to look over and see just how far you've come to this point in your life. The journey is not over, so keep going!

"Stop doubting yourself. Work hard and make it happen, trust the process and keep hustling!"
SUCCESS MINDED

Here's another quote I want to add....

"Stop thinking there's someone more capable or better than you. There's no success in comparison. Be clear about what you want. Focus obsessively on your goals. Work hard. Never quit."
SUCCESS MINDED

I just want you to know your life is not a waste. Your past is not and was not a waste of your time. All that you've experienced can be used to continue to build your future. As long as you place every dilemma, every obstacle, every victory, and goal achieved in its proper place and perspective. Everything has its particular portion of space in your life. The memories, the mistakes, and the mess-ups are all a part of your journey. So, make sure that all of your experiences are the stepping stones and not the stumbling blocks you use to take you to that next level of God's Goodness and Grace for your life.

It's not over; keep going!

Igniting The Leading Lady In You

Dr. Halene Giddens

One More Thing

"There's always one more thing
you can do to increase your odds of success."
HAL MOORE

"Now my beloved ones, I have saved these most
important truths for last: Be supernaturally infused
with strength through your life-union with the Lord
Jesus. Stand victorious with the force of his explosive
power flowing in and through you. Put on God's
complete set of armor provided for us, so that you will
be protected as you fight against the evil strategies of
the accuser! Your hand-to-hand combat is not with
human beings, but with the highest principalities and
authorities operating in rebellion under the heavenly
realms.... Because of this, you must wear all the armor
that God provides so you're protected as you confront
the slanderer, for you are destined <u>for all things and will</u>
<u>rise victorious."</u>
Ephesians 6:10-13 (TPT)
(Underlined words are added by the author for emphasis.)

197

As Leading Ladies, we must remain fit for the fight. I know just reading those few words may make you tired, but do not worry, we're going to discuss a few tools for your fitness needs. I'm not necessarily talking about your workout regimen, though we should probably each have one. I'm talking about staying in this fight to the very finish!

This fight of faith, with your Father in Heaven as your Help, is guaranteed to get you to the finish line! You just have to stay in it and stay with it! No matter how often and how hard the punches fly, you must decide right now that you will remain *"strong in the Lord and in the power of His Might* (Psalm 107:2)!" We declare it to be so!

I love these scriptures in the book of Ephesians in chapter six, Paul writes to the church of Ephesus, and he saved this very *"important truth for last."* The Apostle Paul wants the people of God to understand that their strength and power come from having a *"life union"* and an ongoing continuous relationship with the Lord. This is vitally important to our victory! He explains to win every battle and to have success, you must, as the amplified version of this scripture says, *"be empowered by your union"* with the Lord and *"draw your strength"* from Him.

Fight the good fight of the faith. Take hold of the eternal life to which you were called when you made your good confession in the presence of many witnesses. In the sight of God, who gives life to everything, and of Christ Jesus…
1 Timothy 6:12-13 (NIV)
(Underlined words are added by the author for emphasis.)

In this life we have the privilege of living, we will have
to fight some battles. As I have said before, tests, trials, and
tragedies will inevitably come. Unfortunately, it's what this
world consists of, not in totality, but part of what we will
encounter. But Jesus said we can still live a joyful, happy,
fruitful, fulfilling life due to this significant fact: He has
overcome the world, and that's good news (John 16:33)! His
victory is our victory!

So, don't be in any way discouraged that we must have our
fight stance ready. When we have the Word of God that tells
us we can have unwavering hope and faith in our Heavenly
Father, we will always win! Jesus overcame the enemy and the
awfulness of the world, so you and I can as well!

THE LEADING LADY SURVIVES

Like Gloria Gaynor sang back in the late 70s, "I Will
Survive," that's part of our mantra! With the help of God's
Holy Spirit working in us and with us, we will not only
survive, but we will thrive! This is the overcomer's life! It
doesn't matter how the weapons of this world's warfare are
waged against us; we've got to sing like Destiny's Child, "I'm
a survivor! I'm not gonna give up!" Don't give up, don't give
in, and don't go back! Instead, we must draw strength from
our Life Source, Jesus Christ, and continue to stay and stand
strong in the Lord!

I just had this thought I'd like to emphasize:

This is the Ultimate Survival of the Fittest; You're Fierce and
A Force to be reckoned with! Sister, You Are Graced for the

Grind, and You Are Fit For The Fight!

In this last and final segment, I want to leave you with a few tools for your trade—the trade of living your unbeatable life! Remember this: whatever you may think is stacked up against you, you can overcome it. You've been made to *prosper*! That simply means *to do and be well*. It means you're equipped to conquer; you're unstoppable! So, don't allow the adversary of your soul to stop you from succeeding! There's too much at stake for you to be stopped!

Again, in the book of Ephesians, the Apostle Paul lists the tools we have to be unstoppable! In the King James Version, it's called, *"the whole armor of God!"* When we put on this armor, we saturate our lives with God's Preeminent Word, Presence in and over our lives, and Power working in and through our lives! Conquering at the highest level takes all of this!

"To win the fight, you have to have the right strategy and the right resources, because victories don't come by accident."
MISS CLARA FROM WAR ROOM

My husband and I met back in the 80s while in college, and he used to listen to a rap group called the Beastie Boys. One of their rap songs that was very popular during the time was called "Fight for Your Right." The lyrical hook said, "You gotta fight for your right to party!" While I can certainly agree with that sentiment, depending on the type of party, more importantly, you have to fight for your right to be holy! Yes, I said holy! There are so many things that can take you out of your holiness stance. People may come to you and tell you, "It doesn't take all of that." Take all of what? It doesn't take all of whatever you're doing to remain in a place of holiness with your God.

No one can say what it takes for you and me to be in that holy place with our God. Therefore, whatever it takes is what it takes for me to be a holy woman of God. I can't and won't give that up! But, most significantly, what it takes is that which Paul describes in the Passion Translation as being *"supernaturally infused with strength through your life union with the Lord."* This must be part of your fight stance! Paul continues to describe in Ephesians chapter six what the whole armor of God looks like. Although Paul uses the natural armored suit of a soldier, what he describes is all grounded and founded in the Lord and His Word.

1 Peter 1:15-16 admonishes us to live this holy lifestyle and be holy unto our God because our God is holy. Our Heavenly Father wouldn't encourage us to be something that we absolutely couldn't be. We can be exactly what He's given us the ability to be because He said we could indeed be it! That's exactly what we need to keep up this fight, sometimes every moment of every day. It is the right to be holy and to live holy lives.

We have to fight for our right to live upright before our God. Our Heavenly Father has made each one of us to be salt and light (Matthew 5:13-16). That means our lives are a reflection of God's Love, Light, and Life. As believers in Christ, when we are true reflections of these three aims, we become what keeps the world from going completely catawampus, plain crazy, and mad! Jesus compares our existence as followers of Him here on earth as salt as well as light.

Salt is the preservative that causes meat not to spoil, become putrid, rancid, or to go bad. That is precisely the purpose for our earthly existence when we make the everyday choice to live upright (Proverbs 10:9; Isaiah 33:15-18a). Just our righteous living keeps the forces of evil and wickedness to its full extreme at bay (Matthew 16:18,19)! Yes, people, it could be much, much worse than what we've got going on right now!

Jesus also calls us the light of the world. We're not supposed to hide this light that God has created us to show off because we are truly a reflection of the Son. When we allow the Light of His Love to shine through our lives, we show the world His Healing Light, especially to those around us. So, let that illuminating Light shine in and through you and be an inspiration! We become witnesses of His Goodness (Acts 1:8). It's a part of the gift that our Father has created each of us to be in this world, which can be dark and dismal. You and I, beautiful women of God, and brothers, too, are the salt of the earth and the light of the world (Mark 9:50; Ephesians 5:8-14; Philippians 2:15)!

We must keep God's Peace within us, along with holiness, righteousness, and staying immersed in the Lord by embracing His Holy Word every day, which is how we keep that holy body armor on at all times. One of the tools of our trade that will keep us fit for the fight is finding our place of peace with our Prince of Peace Jesus!

Then, because you belong to Christ Jesus, God will bless
you with peace that no one can completely understand.
And this peace will control the way you think and feel.
Philippians 4:7 (CEV)

Our God, Who gave us Jesus, gives us His Peace that we can't even figure out! That's the kind of Peace that surrounds us in the middle of the greatest storms in our lives. That's the kind of Peace that saturates us from the inside out! That's the kind of Peace that causes us to carry on every single day! That's the kind of Peace that God gives us to make it to the finish line!

YOU CAN HAVE SANCTUARY IN THE SAVIOR'S PRESENCE

Send thee help from the sanctuary,
and strengthen thee out of Zion...
Psalms 20:2 KJV

The Sanctuary is a sacred and holy place. It is a place of peace, protection, and refuge as well as a haven for rest. It's what Quasimodo called out in Disney's adaptation of The Hunchback of Notre Dame, "Sanctuary! Sanctuary!" *In true historical times, anyone wh*o may have been in trouble, guilty or not, could run into any church building and find safety from prosecution and persecution. It was against the law to arrest, persecute, prosecute, hurt, harm, or kill someone who would run into the Sanctuary.

In the Old Testament of the Bible, certain ones would run and take hold of what was called the Horns of the Altar, the place where sacrifices were made by God's people as an outward act of worship. They would give their offerings to the priest of that day, and the priest would place their sacrifice on the Horns of the Altar; it was a holy and sacred act in a holy and sacred place—the Sanctuary. So, if anyone ran to that place and grabbed those horns, they would be safe from harm, hurt, danger, or even what they may have deserved. Thus, they found safety in the Sanctuary (1 Kings 1:50,51).

Whenever life gets too overwhelming or the pressures of your heart and mind become too much to handle, lift your hands to Heaven and yell out, speak out or just murmur to yourself, "Peace be still!" Allow the God of Peace to enter your heart and mind once again to become your sanctuary, your place of rest, peace, and safety. Quasimodo decided to live in the Sanctuary because he was always safe there. You can dwell in that same place of peace and safety right in your heart and mind. Although the physical building that is the Sanctuary is essential to us, it doesn't have to be a physical place, it can be and should also be the condition of your heart. All you have to do is call on the God of Peace, grab hold of Him, and don't ever let go!

*"Peace brings with it so many positive emotions
that it is worth aiming for in all circumstances."*
ESTELLE ELIOT

This place of peace is a level of trust found in knowing your Savior, Jesus Christ. He is the Place of Peace because He is the Prince of our Peace. The Word of God states with clarity in Psalm 20:2 that we can receive help by entering into the Sanctuary. It also says we can become strengthened out of Zion, the physical place in the city of Jerusalem where God's people went to worship Him. Entering into the Sanctuary of our Holy God allows you and me to have a weekly or semiweekly collective experience with our God, according to our westernized civilization. In the easternized culture, the people of God would go daily to the House of God to pray and worship (Mark 14:49, Luke 19:47, Acts 2:46).

Other versions of Psalm 20:2 elaborate on the fact that we can receive supernatural help from His Sanctuary and receive support and be refreshed from Zion. We can receive so many benefits from entering into the Sanctuary, which is found in the House of God! In the Sanctuary, we are changed and charged to continue to live a life of healing, health, hope, wholeness, and holiness. We can live this life in this awesome manner because of the Holy One Who lives in us! We receive fuel for the fight, the means, and the might to keep going! When we get to that Sacred Place, we obtain that much-needed pick-me-up for our daily living!

Another tool for your trade that's a part of your fitness needs, which keeps you fit for this fight, is joy.

JOY: AN INSIDE JOB

Our late Apostle Holcomb taught a message about the joy of the Lord and how that joy is an inside job. To have the true benefits and qualities of joy, it has to start on the inside. How can we enjoy life or anything else for that matter if joy isn't in us? So, in our hearts, minds, and disposition in how we live, joy has to be on the inside to be experienced on the outside. It's the premise of the word enjoy. To *enjoy* means *to take pleasure in; to experience joy*. It's a combination of two words: *en* and *joy*. So, by simple implication, the prefix *en* that comes before the word *joy* predisposes that to experience joy, it must start on the inside of you and me.

Your words were found, and I ate them, And Your word was to me the joy and rejoicing of my heart; For I am called by Your name, O LORD God of hosts.
Jeremiah 15:16 (NKJV)

Joy is an experience we partake in, a pleasure that starts with enjoying the Word of God. The Prophet Jeremiah said when *"I found Your words and I ate them, it was to me the joy and the rejoicing of my heart."* Through all the horrible persecution he faced, Jeremiah found inner joy again and again because he continued to consume God's Word. He was able to rejoice in his heart over and over again, although trouble kept coming to him. To rejoice is a choice that we can make for ourselves in even the darkest of times! To rejoice means to experience and embrace joy time after time.

This consumption of the Word of God is a spiritual endeavor that comes from a natural perspective. It was a lesson taught early on in the Jewish culture. In those early days, the spiritual leaders would allow the children to eat the

Word of God. They would dip the scrolls, a roll of parchment paper, which contained the written Word of God, in honey. Nowadays, according to Bible Belt Jewish Culture, they may print what's known as the Torah alphabet on little squares of chocolate, still signifying that the Word of God is good and yummy. Prior to this though, they would ingest the scrolls or lick the honey off of the scrolls as a reminder that the Word of God is sweet to the soul (Psalm 19:7,10; Psalm 119:103; Proverbs 16:24; Ezekiel 3:1-3).

The Word of God has to be a sustainer to our souls! It satisfies our hungry hearts when we need it, and it produces that joy in our most difficult moments. Whenever we open the scrolls, the Scriptures, we should be reminded that this Word is good for us and good to us every time we take it in—first allowing God's Word to work on the inside then allowing the fruit of the Word to show up on the outside! Just like in the Jewish culture, starting with the children, we have to practice letting the Word of God taste good to us on the inside.

You know the song we like to quote and sing, "This joy that I have the world didn't give it and the world can't take it away." Yes, we sing that and say that. Yet, the simplest, tiniest, minute little things can steal our joy every day! Our jobs, career or the lack thereof, spouse and children or the lack thereof, money, bills, and the cashier in the grocery store all have the propensity to steal our joy. The person driving slowly in the fast lane, or vice versa, whipping by fast in the slow lane, can steal our joy. All these things can distract us, stunt, cripple, stifle and even cut off and cut out our joy. That's why joy must take root on the inside of us to do the job that keeps us full of joy.

---

*Then he said to them, "Go your way. Eat the fat and
drink sweet wine and send portions to anyone who has
nothing ready, for this day is holy to our Lord. And do
not be grieved, for <u>the joy of the Lord is your strength</u>."*
Nehemiah 8:10 ESV

(Underlined words are added by the author for emphasis.)

Nehemiah was a simple man of God, enslaved in exile as
the King of Persia's cupbearer, who exclusively served wine
to the king. After hearing of the destruction of his home,
Nehemiah had a strong desire to rebuild the dilapidated and
torn down walls of his native land Jerusalem. He was able to
obtain favor with the king, King Artaxerxes, mainly due to
God's favor on his life and of course, his good relationship with
the king himself. Let me pause right here to say that when we
employ joy by allowing it to work inside of us, regardless of
our outer experiences or inner turmoils, this joy causes us to
handle ourselves in a way that appeals to others around us!

Nehemiah would not have found this type of favor with
this king if he hadn't behaved himself wisely in the king's
presence! That's for sure! The Scriptures read that he never
had a sad countenance in the presence of the king unless he
was sick. He always kept himself in the place of being pleasant
to be around. How else could he have been the very one to
serve wine to the king? I know that may seem like a minuscule
thing to you and me, but way back then, it was pretty huge!
As a result, Nehemiah received favor to go and take care of the
broken-down walls of Jerusalem. He was given letters from

the king to pick up all the materials he needed to make this endeavor happen.

Nehemiah persevered through opposition. He led the Israelite people to reconstruct and stabilize the walls of that city. As a result, many of the children of Israel were able to go back to Jerusalem to live once again in their own country with their people. As they returned to live and reestablish their lives, they also brought back and reaffirmed the teachings they lived by, found in God's Holy Word. When they heard the word, realizing that they hadn't been serving God nor following His instructions found in His Word, they were ashamed, saddened, depressed, and began to cry bitterly! That is where this scripture reads in Nehemiah 8:10, *"the joy of the Lord is your strength."*

But Nehemiah, who was a modest, unassuming man of God with a heart to return to his homeland and bring God's people back to the place of serving Him, said, "Hey, it's ok! It's time to celebrate! We're back, we're back in the place of our home, and even though we've suffered difficult times because of our wrong choices, the joy of the Lord is our strength!" And that's something to be exceedingly glad about! Being an inside job, joy isn't predicated on what's going on around us or what we may be experiencing on the inside of us.

As long as we're living on this side of life, there's always going to be something in this world, in the nation, in our state, city, and right in our own homes that can be or go wrong. But no matter how life hits us, and it sometimes can hit us pretty hard, we have to remind ourselves when the most difficult circumstances come to interrupt our lives to pull up and pull out the joy of the Lord. Because joy is an inside job, and the joy of the Lord is how we receive our strength.

So, we've got to say and sing it like we mean it! I've got the joy, joy, joy, joy down in my heart, down in my heart today, and to stay!

There are many tools of the trade that will keep you fit for the fight, lovely Leading Lady. We just need to employ them. These tools are never far from us; they are right by our side. All we need to do is reach for them and be empowered by them! Honestly, this entire book is meant to help you with that very endeavor! As we started in this segment with the scripture found in Ephesians 6:13, *"for you are destined for all things and you will rise victorious!"* That is you, Leading Lady! This is most definitely you!

THE LEADING LADY SOARS

---

but those who hope in the LORD will renew their strength. They will soar on wings like eagles; they will run and not grow weary, they will walk and not be faint.
Isaiah 40:31 (NIV)

Leading Lady, you were meant to *soar*. When we amplify that word, some of the synonyms are *to arise, to ascend*, and *aspire upward*. This is your journey—to go up! Your journey is to expand your horizon and experience to reach your full potential! The way to accomplish this task, or another way of saying it, the way to take flight is to continue to have your faith renewed and strength built up in the Lord!

Yes, there may be forces that oppose your success, but the Word of God proclaims when the enemy rises against you, the Spirit of the Lord will lift up a Standard against him (Isaiah 59:19). Another version of this scripture says that as a result of the Messiah's Intervention, when the enemy comes to assault you, the Spirit of the Lord will come in like a rushing force to stop the enemy's attack! Oh my goodness! You really are unbeatable! You can't lose with the weapons God gives you to win every battle! With God on your side, lifting His Force Shield around you, you are more than a conqueror (Romans 8:7)!

> *"If we never had the courage to take the leap of faith, we'd be cheating God out of a chance to mount us up with wings like eagles and watch us soar!"*
> JEN STEPHENS

Because, Leading Lady, you are destined and predetermined by God to succeed, you will rise victorious! That's God's Promise for you! With our hope firmly anchored in the Lord (Hebrews 6:19), it's the reason we can always be prepared for every battle, and it's how we win!

Leading Lady, you've been given the tools for your trade to make an indelible mark on your corner of the world! Remember, there is absolutely no insignificant contribution, no gift too small, no word spoken that can't be life-changing to the hearer. I pray the purpose that our God has created for you will burn in you until you reach for it and fulfill it! I sure hope you've been Ignited because you are God's gift to your generation!

Igniting The Leading Lady In You

Works Cited

The American Heritage Dictionary of English Language (2000). Boston: Houghton Mifflin

Kendall, R. K., Strong, J., and Kendall, R., 2001, The New Strong's Expanded Dictionary of Bible Words, Thomas Nelson Publishers.

Strong, J., 2001, The New Strong's Expanded Dictionary of Bible Words: Hebrew and Greek Dictionaries, Thomas Nelson Publishers.

Oxford English Dictionary, Oxford University Press, September 2021.

Igniting The Leading Lady In You

About The Author

D r. Halene Marie Giddens is the First Lady of Destiny Christian Center, located in Victorville, California. She and her husband, Bishop Jesse Giddens, have been married for over 34 years. The two of them have been in full-time ministry together over 26 years. They have two adult children, Brittney Halene Marie and Jonathan David.

Dr. Halene is a licensed and ordained minister of the Gospel. She received her bachelor's degree in Biblical Studies from Speak the Word School of Ministry in 1996, her Master's Degree in Theology from the Institute of Teaching God's Word in 1998, and her Doctorate of Ministry from the Minnesota Graduate School of Theology in 2005. She, along with her husband, Bishop Giddens, completed the Sonship School of the Firstborn under the tutelage of the late Apostle Nathaniel Holcomb, who recently transitioned to be with the Lord, and their spiritual mother, Pastor Valerie Ivy Holcomb in 2007.

She is a sought-after speaker at women's conferences,

seminars, and churches. She is anointed and has been appointed to speak the Word in due season to them that are weary. Dr. Halene also established the Women With Destiny (WWD) and Daughters of Destiny Ministries, where both are geared toward Christian women's spiritual health and development.

She says, "It is a privilege and honor to be able to share the life-changing Word of God with God's people." Most importantly, she truly loves the One she preaches about, Who is Jesus Christ, the Son of the Living God.

Dr. Halene says of her life that she has learned to trust in the Lord her God and encourages others to seek and sustain an intimate walk with Christ. She enjoys being alongside her husband in ministry and wouldn't have it any other way.

Destiny Christian Center

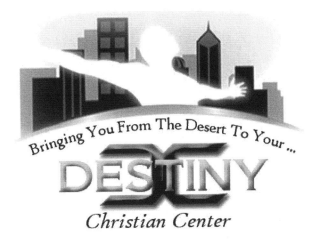

For more information about Destiny Christian Center, speaking engagements,
or additional resources, please contact us by:

Address
14380 Amargosa Rd.
Victorville, California 92392

Phone 760-951-8500
www.destinychristiancenter.org

We look forward to hearing from you soon.

Igniting The Leading Lady In You